19-11

In Plane View

In this age of space and air
travel a new vocabulary has been born
and a new culture has been created.
"Thrust" has replaced "horsepower."
Through the miracle of air travel,
businessmen commute hundreds of miles
to their offices. The Jet Set crosses
the continent to see a show or attend a
party. Sonic booms shatter windows and
flight paths shatter nerves.

This airborne culture needs a witness
of Christ in its own language. The crews
of the gigantic silver ships of the skies
must hear of God's love and grace
in a manner that will be both appealing
and familiar.

In *Come Fly With Me,* this witness is given
and the story of God's redemptive love
is presented in a "plane view" for the
people who vie with the birds, and to
whom the skyways are as familiar as the
streets of their hometown.

COME FLY with ME

by Lane G. Adams

Illustrated by Jeffrey Wilson

A Division of G/L Publications
Glendale, California, U.S.A.

51421

The publishers do not necessarily endorse the entire contents of all publications referred to in this book.

Scripture quotations, other than the King James Version, are from the following sources:
The Living Bible Paraphrased (Wheaton, Ill.: Tyndale House Publishers, 1971). Used by permission.
The New Berkeley Version in Modern English (Grand Rapids, Mich.: Zondervan Publishing House, fourth printing, paperback edition, 1971). Used by permission.
Today's English Version of the New Testament (© American Bible Society, 1966, paperback edition). Used by permission.

© Copyright 1973 by Lane G. Adams
Printed in U.S.A.
All rights reserved.

Published by
Regal Books Division, G/L Publications
Glendale, California 91209, U.S.A.
Library of Congress Catalog Card No. 73-79843
ISBN 0-8307-0253-9

Contents

Foreword

Lane Adams has been a trusted and fruitful associate of mine for nine years, during which period he has conducted forty city-wide crusades in the United States, Canada, England, Australia and New Zealand. He came to our evangelistic team after having been the founding minister of the highly effective Key Biscayne Presbyterian Church of Miami, Florida, and pastor of the Cedar Springs Presbyterian Church of Knoxville, Tennessee.

I first came to know Lane Adams as a special team member during our New York Crusade of 1957. Lane and his wife, Annette, took a leave of absence from Columbia Theological Seminary to work among people of New York's show-business community, to contact them for Jesus Christ. Lane's experience as a nightclub singer had prepared him well for communicating with that special segment of our society. As a result of this work, he and Jerome Hines, Metropolitan opera star, founded the Christian Arts Fellowship.

This fascinating book grows out of Lane's varied experiences as a fighter pilot in World War II and the rough experiences that come to any young man in war time. One of these traumatic experiences is called by airmen, "vertigo." Lane takes this condition of physical vertigo and draws a parallel to the spiritual state of mankind. Vertigo is thinking you are right side up when you are really upside down. Lane writes interestingly of the physical malady, and forcefully of the more dangerous spiritual malady of being totally disoriented. He gives the biblical-Christian solution. Unless a pilot comes out of vertigo, he will crash. Unless the individual comes out of his spiritual vertigo, he is in chaos without knowing what his problem is.

With a fresh approach to an age-old problem, Lane Adams tells people of their plight. If you are troubled, possibly your problem is vertigo. As you go through the pages of this book—which I highly commend for your reading—you can diagnose your problem and take the prescription for its cure.

The publication of this book coincides with the commencement of a new ministry for Lane as he leaves our team to become Minister of Evangelism for the famous Hollywood Presbyterian Church in Hollywood, California. My friendship, prayers and eager encouragement go with him into this exciting new work.

Billy Graham
Montreat, N.C.
April 16, 1973

Preface

Many books have been written for the "man in the street." This book has been written for people "up in the air," both in the literal and/or spiritual sense of that phrase. Flying has become commonplace for more and more people. Yet, apart from pilots, very few know much about what actually makes a plane get off the ground, or what keeps it in the air.

The relationship between the principle of flight and the principle of the Christian gospel has always intrigued me. The exciting experience of flight is more than matched by the experience of having Jesus Christ lift you into new life on a higher "plane." I know of nothing that illustrates that new life quite as well as flying. Almost all of the flying illustrations in this book are drawn from my own experience as a pilot or passenger. I offer this book with a desire to be technical enough to intrigue flyers and yet simple enough to interest those who are not.

My prayer is that this book might be used by God to speak to you about His great love, and lead you to experience that glorious lift-off to life on an undreamed-of plane of fulfillment.

The list of all who have encouraged me in this venture is too long to be included here, but I do want to express appreciation to those who helped in special ways. The editorial assistance of Mr. Terry M. Moore, my son-in-law, was crucial in getting me off dead center on a manuscript half-done, and pushing me on to completion. The typing and encouragement of Mrs. Eleanor Sykes, and the patience of her husband Bill deserve special mention. Mr. B. Ray Thompson's generous assistance finally made it all happen.

Lane Adams

Getting Off the Ground

CHAPTER 1

There wasn't much airplane to shake, but what there was, vibrated and shook almost as much as I did. I had known the moment for that first solo flight was imminent, but I had no idea that it was going to come so soon. The instructor surprised me by stepping out of the plane several flight hours before the schedule prescribed, and now I was alone in the little Piper Cub. I taxied the plane to the end of the lumpy grass field, checked the one trim tab for proper setting, took a deep breath, and applied full power. As the plane began its jouncing roll down the runway, everything seemed so much more frightening without the safe figure of the instructor sitting in front of me. *"Get the tail up! Keep the nose straight! Bring that right wing level!"* Nobody was calling out these orders at me now, yet I heard every command and obeyed.

Then it just happened! I was in the air! Free from

the earth! The banging noise of the bounding wheels stopped, and only the engine's roar remained. Gently I pulled the nose up, clearing the trees at the end of the runway by a good margin.

I had done it! I was flying! Slowly, the earth dropped away; cows and houses and barns grew smaller. I turned forty-five degrees left, then right, and I was out of the traffic pattern. The little plane obeyed my every command. *I* was doing it. I was flying—all by myself—I was up!

Those of us who have experienced this thrill of self-piloted flight can appreciate the inexpressible exhilaration of leaving the earth behind—to fly like the birds—to soar, to wheel, to roll, to dive, to light again.

For thousands of years man looked helplessly with envy and longing at the soaring birds. If only there was some way to break his earth-binding shackles and fly; but the pull of gravity pinned man to the earth. Failure in his first efforts to fly did not kill his desire. Not having been endowed by his Creator with the necessary flying equipment, man studied the birds and began to work on supplying himself with the two things necessary for flight—a *wing* and *power*.

Of man's eternal urge to fly, Douglas D. Bond says, "Flying has long held a special place in man's thinking. It has been associated with aspiration and freedom from the restrictions of earth or of reality and has had strong religious connotations as well."[1]

Even as man has stood rooted to the earth and dreamed of flying, at the same time, he has always been able to dream of living on a higher level of honor, dedication, purity and selflessness; far beyond anything he has ever been able to actualize in his own life. Man can think so much better than he can do. Like James Thurber's Walter Mitty, in his mind, he soars to heights of bravery, daring and accomplishment, only to be yanked back with a thud to reality. Alas, his clay feet are bound to a much humbler level of very ordinary achievement. This great gap between aspiration and accomplishment is the more frustrating because man dreams of soaring, and still has to tread the pedestrian way. Bound to his earthiness, man can yet yearn for the power to live closer to the level of his highest aspirations.

But how does he get off the ground? Physically speaking, man has learned to fly. Can he also spiritually learn to fly? We've always been able to take mental flights to dizzying altitudes. But in personal and corporate conduct we remain stuck in the mud of the earth. When one compares science and philosophy books with history books, the staggering gap between how high we can think and how low we perform becomes immediately obvious. In commenting on the sad history of human behavior, natural scientist Konrad Lorenz speculates on how we might appear to an absolutely unbiased investigator from another planet. He suggests, "If—our Martian naturalist knew of the explosive rise in human populations, the ever-increasing destructiveness of weapons, and the division of mankind into a few political camps, he would not expect the future of humanity to be more rosy than that of several hostile clans of rats on a ship almost devoid of food."[2]

Like a spiritual law of gravity, sin continues to pull man downward. Sin frustrates his yearning to fly his life at the level of his highest aspirations.

The principles of aerodynamics, which first lifted man off the earth, come as something of a shock and surprise when they are first understood. The diagram below is a cutaway section of a simple wing.

You will notice that the bottom side of the wing is almost flat, whereas the top side of the wing is curved. The distance from A to B over the top of the wing is considerably longer than the distance from A to B under the bottom side of the wing. Why? Well, as the wing is thrust through the air by the source of power (the engine) a curious thing occurs. As the wing splits the air, it is obvious that the part of the air which goes over the top of the wing has a greater distance to travel than that part of the air which goes under the bottom of the wing. Since there is no such thing as a perfect vacuum, the air going over the top must make its trip to the trailing edge of the wing at B much faster than the air going under the bottom. According to Bernoulli's principle, the increase of the speed of the air over a surface calls for a corresponding decrease in pressure. Because the air over the top of the wing is traveling faster than the air under the bottom of the wing, the air pressure on the top is considerably less than the air pressure on the bottom. Therefore, the plane is literally sucked off the ground by this decrease in pressure on the top of the wing. Most people are startled to discover that approximately two-thirds of the lift in takeoff comes from the top of the wing and only one-third from the bottom. When enough speed is provided thrusting the wing through the air, sufficient lift results, overcoming the pull of gravity, freeing one from the earth and resulting in the glorious excitement of flying.

But suppose a wing were put on a plane upside down. No matter how fast you thrust the wing through the air, it would only press the plane more surely to the earth, because with the long side of the wing faced toward the earth, it then would cooperate with the law of gravity and hold the plane down. Greater speed would mean nothing but certainty of remaining earth bound.

Put the wing on the plane properly, with the long side pointed heavenward, and flight becomes possible.

The Bible says all of us are born with our spiritual wings on upside down. If you imagine your life like the cutaway diagram of the wing, you will see what I mean. The long side of our lives is toward the earth, that is, the world. It isn't that we don't have part of our being looking heavenward, but this part represents merely the short side of our lives.

We think about God, even acknowledge the possibility of His existence, and go through periodic ritual observance of these beliefs. In contrast to this, moreover, the long side of ourselves is aimed toward the earth and not toward the heavens. No matter how much religious speed we get up (going to church, being busy in doing good things and the like) we are still earth-bound because the major share of our attention is directed toward things other than God.

The Word of God invites you to consider this: "You want to get off the ground spiritually?" Then, "Set your affections on things *above*, not on things on the earth."³ The Lord Jesus said, "Seek ye *first* the kingdom of God, and his righteousness; and all these things shall be added unto you."⁴ "And God spake . . . saying, . . . Thou shalt have no other gods before me."⁵ In order to get off the ground spiritually you must have your priorities rearranged. God wants the place of first affection, first allegiance, and first obedience in your life. God wants your primary attention both in quality and quantity. And He demands that kind of relationship daily. He has much to say to you, and He is interested in what you say to Him. But this takes time, and for you to give time to this initially and continually demands a determined act of your will every day. *I will* put God first! *I will* make His priorities mine. He says, "The things which are seen are temporal; but the things which are not seen are eternal,"⁶ therefore, relying on His strength *I will* set my affections on things that are above.

It isn't that you don't have a side of your wing

facing toward the world (the earth). A wing isn't one-sided—it has two sides, but the long side of the wing is facing toward the earth. There are the matters of making a living, raising children, developing your family and friends, and getting on in this world. Attention and time must be given to these things. But they may no longer be allowed to occupy primary or ultimate positions of concern to you, for God demands that the short side of your life be toward the world and that the long side be directed toward the Lord, giving Him the primary place in everything.

Incredible as it sounds, when a man gives God and His Word the primary place of obedient attention he will experience the excitement of a glorious spiritual lift-off that will free him to climb to levels of personal conduct and accomplishment he never dreamed possible. Knowing this, the prophet Isaiah exults, "They that wait upon the Lord . . . shall mount up with wings as eagles. . . ."[1]

Your next question might very well be, "These are all very nice words, but what do I have to do to get off the ground spiritually and rise above the level of existence that I now know? What is the first step that I take toward setting my affections on those things which are above?"

The most crucial thing involved in both physical and spiritual "lift-off" is the word *commitment*. A man must first be committed to the idea of flying. Then he must commit himself completely to the instrument designed to lift him off the surface of the earth.

So the man who wants to experience a spiritual

"lift-off," must be committed to the idea that God is offering to him, freely, the opportunity to rise against the gravitational pull of sin that has always kept his feet mired in the earth. As a pilot must be committed to the idea of leaving the earth in order to know the joys of flying, so the believer must recognize that, in order to rise above where he is, there are many things of this world that are going to have to be left behind.

As the pilot commits himself completely to the plane, so also must the believer commit himself to the person of Jesus Christ. It is in Him that we can take off into a whole new dimension of life. The Bible puts it this way, "But God is so rich in mercy; he loved us so much that even though we were spiritually dead and doomed by our sins, he gave us back our lives again when he raised Christ from the dead—only by his undeserved favor have we ever been saved—and lifted us up from the grave into glory along with Christ, where we sit with him in the heavenly realms—all because of what Christ Jesus did."[8]

Earlier we said that man had to devise a wing and power in order to accomplish flight. If then the wing is provided by getting one's priorities in order and putting Jesus Christ foremost in his life, where then comes the power? The source of the power is God Himself. Jesus said, "All *power* is given unto me in heaven and in earth."[9] The apostle John says, "But as many as received him (Jesus Christ), to them gave he *power* to become the sons of God, even to them that believe on his name."[10] And Paul goes on: "For it is *God* which worketh in you both

10

to will and to do of his good pleasure."[11] ". . . You will be filled with his mighty, glorious *strength* so that you can keep going no matter what happens— always full of the joy of the Lord . . .".[12] ". . . I can do it only because Christ's mighty energy is at work within me."[13]

The means that God uses to communicate His power to us is His Word, the Bible. Jesus said, "Man shall not live by bread alone, but by every word that proceedeth out of the mouth of God."[14] As physical energy is generated by physical food, so spiritual energy is generated by spiritual food. The source of this energy is the Word of God. As man must obtain daily quantities of good food in order to have physical energy, so he must avail himself of spiritual energy through spiritual food. Jesus said, "The words that I speak unto you, they are spirit, and they are life."[15] The combination of the spiritual power and spiritual wing available in Jesus Christ can raise us to a new level we never dreamed possible, and so Paul says, ". . . Whether a person has Christ is what matters, and he is equally available to all."[16]

Perhaps it would be well to add a word of caution: Every aircraft has its load limits. Load it beyond what the manufacturer recommends and you will never get it off the ground. A good pilot is always conscious of this and remains well within the limitations specified.

Many have failed to accomplish a spiritual take-off because they exceeded the load limits of the MANUFACTURER and tried to carry too much of the world with them. The Bible says, "Let us lay

11

aside every weight, and the sin which doth so easily beset us . . .".[11] There are some things that simply have to be left behind. It isn't that God can't lift them, but that He won't. This is what repentance is all about—being willing to drop those things that you know to be displeasing to God. I didn't need anyone to tell me; I knew from the beginning those things that had to be left behind. I suspect you know, too, don't you?

The story is told of an old farmer in the early days of flying, in whose cow pasture a barnstorming pilot landed his plane. Looking over the rickety craft the farmer "allowed as how" he didn't believe the blamed thing could lift him off the ground. Finally persuaded by the pilot to try a free ride, he took off and for the first time got a plane view of his entire farm, at one time. Safely back on the ground the pilot said to his exhilarated passenger, "See, I told you it could lift you off the ground and fly you around!" To which the old farmer gravely shook his head, spit on the ground, and said, "Still don't know for sure about that, Sonny! You see, I never put my full weight down!"

Well, my friend, you can put your full weight down on the sure promise of God. If you want a plane view of God—and life, love and hope—than set your affections on the things which are above. Receive Jesus Christ as Saviour and Lord, and experience that mysterious drawing power from above that can lift you off to a new level of hope, and that can bring all of life, at its best, into plane view.

This is not to imply that the true Christian life is

one of endlessly serene and problem-free progress.
The Christian life and flying are full of surprises.
Some of them can be downright hairy.

Notes

1. Douglas D. Bond, M.D.; Professor of Psychiatry, *The Love and Fear of Flying,* (New York: International Universities Press, Inc., 1952), p. 15.
2. Konrad Lorenz, *On Aggression,* (New York: Harcourt Brace and World, Inc., 1967), pp. 229-230.
3. Colossians 3:2, *King James Version*
4. Matthew 6:33, *KJV*
5. Exodus 20:1,3, *KJV*
6. II Corinthians 4:18, *KJV*
7. Isaiah 40:31, *KJV*
8. Ephesians 2:4-6, *The Living Bible*
9. Matthew 28:18, *KJV*
10. John 1:12, *KJV*
11. Philippians 2:13, *KJV*
12. Colossians 1:11, *TLB*
13. Colossians 1:29, *TLB*
14. Matthew 4:4, *KJV*
15. John 6:63, *KJV*
16. Colossians 3:11, *TLB*
17. Hebrews 12:1, *KJV*

Fasten Your Seat Belts, Please!

CHAPTER 2

It was a rather typical Friday-afternoon crowd on the plane that lifted off from LaGuardia Airport on that hot spring day. One could tell that most on board were veterans as far as travel was concerned: executives, salesmen, technicians, government workers and others traveling for their companies or causes. Some knew each other. The general relief of going home was making for free conversation, while the stewardesses hurried up and down the aisles delivering cocktails and highballs. It seemed more like a commuter train bound for the suburbs than an airliner headed for Washington. The captain had turned off the seat-belt sign and the smokers were turning the cabin blue as, one after another, they fired up. Outside, the sun shone brightly and clouds appeared in the distance.

The sledge-hammer blow from above was as if some mad giant had smashed his clenched fist down on the top of the plane with a crashing sound. The plane plummeted hundreds of feet in seconds. The stewardess rose crazily to the ceiling! People

shot out of their seats! Those who were belted in watched their drinks slush upwards out of their glasses! Now an equally ferocious blow caught the plane from the bottom! The stewardess was crumpled back into the aisle, people were banged back into their seats, and by now the overhead racks were virtually emptied of coats and other smaller items. Instinctively, I shot a glance out at the wings and was surprised to see that they were still intact. We endured yet one more resounding blow from above and then leveled out into turbulence of a less severe nature. The captain apologized, but indicated he'd had no warning. Only now was the plane beginning to move into the clouds I had seen in the distance. In spite of the fact that we flew the rest of the way to Washington through line storms, we never again encountered the severity of turbulence that had hit us in the clear air. We had been victims of the CAT. Some victims never live to tell about it.

Clear Air Turbulence. The CAT. Turbulence in the air has usually been associated with storm clouds, but when planes began flying high enough to get into the jet streams, this new phenomenon was discovered. Storm clouds will show up on radar, and in daytime they can be seen visually; but there is no way yet known to detect clear air turbulence, except by running into it and then sounding a warning to other planes that there is turbulence in the area.

In similar fashion, I wish to issue a warning to all Christians everywhere to *fasten your seat belts, please!* There is turbulence ahead whether you can see it or not! To all who have experienced that

18

glorious spiritual lift-off, I say, "Fasten your seat belts, please."

There seems to be a general misunderstanding abroad to the effect that a real Christian is someone who doesn't have any problems, difficulties, or tragedies to contend with, as other people do. The idea conveyed is that a "victorious Christian" (whatever that is) is a person who always walks around with a big toothy smile on his face indicating that he's got life licked, including all its *problems*. An even more insidious wrinkle on this same theme implies that if this "real Christian" does have problems, it is because there is something drastically wrong with his relationship to Christ; or that he is hiding some deep, dark and mysterious sin that needs confessing.

It doesn't take the new Christian long to acquire this erroneous picture. He observes that not many other Christians are admitting to having any difficulties in their marriages, or with their kids; or that they are fighting temptation or discouragement. So he learns to cover up, too, and begins to feel like the world's biggest hypocrite. He is quite sure that he is the only one who believes in Christ and still manages to run into all kinds of turbulence in his life. Well, to any of you who feel this way I say, "Welcome to the club." You have plenty of company. "The good man does not escape all troubles—he has them too. But the Lord helps him in each and every one."[1]

Sin, like a turbulent cloud, is most usually the visible and understandable reason to fasten your seat belts. But it must be admitted that, like clear air

19

turbulence, there are tragic events which can hit our lives and the lives of others, for which one cannot find either a visible or understandable cause.

Not uncommonly people say to me, "Explain to us why the innocent suffer, why people are starving to death, why there is cancer. Tell us why there is war, and why babies are born deformed. Perhaps we might believe in your God of love if we knew the answers." I have no glib or facile words of explanation for these events.

Time and again the Bible struggles with this subject of unexplainable tragedy, offering some help, but always ending short of a fully satisfying answer to the problem. The Lord Jesus was once asked to explain the incredibly inhuman horror which Pilate perpetrated, when he dismembered some Jewish worshipers in the Temple and mixed their bodies with the animals which they had brought. Pilate then sacrificed the whole lot. What an opportunity to expound on the depravity of man as represented in Pontius Pilate! But Jesus' piercing answer was, "Do you think they were worse sinners than other men from Galilee? . . . Is that why they suffered? Not at all! And don't you realize that you also will perish unless you leave your evil ways and turn to God?" He went on, "And what about the eighteen men who died when the tower of Siloam fell on them? Were they the worst sinners in Jerusalem? Not at all! And you, too, will perish unless you repent."[2]

They had brought up a tragedy for which there was a visible cause, Pontius Pilate. But Jesus brought up a tragedy for which there was no visible cause, either in the character of the people who perished or in the collapse of an impersonal tower. It was easier to offer an answer to the first tragedy than the second, but He seems to have offered an explanation for neither. What did He mean by that puzzling reply, "And you, too, will perish unless you repent"? Perhaps Jesus was saying, "Unless you change the evil inside yourself over which you *have* control, how will you ever accept those evil events outside of yourself over which you have no control?"

It may well be that Jesus also is demanding a more honest sense of proportion in viewing evil in the world. Unexplainable tragedies, like the collapse of the tower of Siloam or any natural disasters, make up such a tiny percentage of the evil in this world, while man's inhumanity to man is directly responsible for all the rest of humanity's suffering and exploitation. Why then stumble over the lesser evil and ignore the greater? Solve, first, the larger sin problem within, before trying to understand the place of natural disaster without.

While it must be admitted, in honesty, that conversion to Jesus Christ does not guarantee a rational explanation for the clear air turbulence of natural disaster, it does introduce you to the absolute goodness in the character of God. This leads one to be able to trust God because of what He is, rather than trusting Him because of explainable circumstances. The National Weather Service states that ninety to ninety-five percent of all serious turbulence is caused by clouds, and that only five to ten percent fits into that mysterious category, clear air turbulence. Surely the same proportions, or greater, apply to the cause of evil in this world. Could any reasoning mind reject God because of five to ten percent of life's events which cannot be explained? The believer learns to trust the good character of God with that mysterious ten percent. He also trusts that God is able to work "*all* things . . . together for good to them that love (Him), to them who are the called according to his purpose."³

Since the visible clouds of human sin cause ninety to ninety-five percent of the turbulence in life, let's put our attention to where the major problem lies. As a matter of fact, Jesus warned His disciples that they could expect trouble *because* they had believed in Him as Lord and Saviour. He said, "If they hated Me, then you can expect that they will hate you!" He warned of severe turbulence in their lives, but He also promised them that He would be with them and give them the strength to endure whatever godless men could cook up.

Paul testifies that this was the case in his life. He even begins his second letter to the Corinthians by saying, "I think you ought to know . . . about the hard time we went through in Asia . . . that we despaired even of life itself."⁴ In chapter 11 of the same letter, he itemizes some of the difficulties he endured. That list is enough to curl your hair. But in the opening chapter he lets us know in advance that he sees a reason for all the troubles. Having had such experiences himself, he is able to report to us how God has met his need, and that He can be depended on to meet our need under similar suffering. These difficulties revealed to him the marvelous character of God in the comfort he received, thus causing him to love God more.

Peter testifies to the same thing. He writes: "There is wonderful joy ahead, even though the going is rough for a while down here. These trials are only to test your faith, to see whether or not it is strong and pure. It is being tested as fire tests gold and purifies it—and your faith is far more precious to God than mere gold; so if your faith remains strong after being tried in the test tube of fiery trials, it will bring you much praise and glory and honor on the day of his return."[5] How much easier it is to pass the tests when you are forewarned that they are coming, and that the God who loves you has a purpose in them. Peter says not to think it strange when trials arise.

We live in a sinful world, and that world's continuing violation of the commandments of God guarantees a turbulent society in which to live. Misguided Christians have tried to avoid the impact of the sin of others by backing off from this world behind monastic walls, or by otherwise isolating and insulating themselves. They soon discover, as Martin Luther did, that the Devil authors this disobedience, and that he can climb monastery walls. It should be obvious to all that the rejection of God and His authority, as well as the rejection of human authority, is bound to have a social effect. Hatred and killing, lying and stealing, immorality and covetousness make for rough going anywhere and anytime, under any kind of political regime. Jesus said that His disciples would be in this world, but that they would not be of it.[6] The tranquility of the Christian's flight through this life is going to be jolted from time to time by the turbulent sin in the world.

But that probably will not jolt him half as much as the sin in himself. It's laughable that we even dare to say, "No one is perfect." Implied is the idea that some of us have come close to perfection but just missed it by a hair. The Apostle John wrote to a group of Christians, "If we say that we have no sin, we are only fooling ourselves, and refusing to accept the truth. . . . If we claim we have not sinned, we are lying and calling God a liar, for he says we have sinned."[7]

Paul spelled out the Christian's situation clearly when he wrote, "For we naturally love to do evil things that are just the opposite from the things that the Holy Spirit tells us to do; and the good things we want to do when the Spirit has his way with us are just the opposite of our natural desires. These two forces within us are constantly fighting each other to win control over us, and our wishes are never free from their pressures."[8] It almost seems too simple to say that the Christian only has to decide which of these two forces he intends to cooperate with in his life, to determine whether he is going to be faced with ongoing turbulence or peace. To whatever degree he follows the Holy Spirit, to that degree he will know love, joy, peace, patience, kindness, goodness, faithfulness, gentleness and self-control. To follow the lower nature a large percentage of the time will produce increasingly rough going.

For the Christian, even that rough going shows the kindness and love of God. How? The writer to the Hebrews explains: ". . . Have you quite forgotten the encouraging words God spoke to you, his child? He said, 'My son, don't be angry when the Lord punishes you. Don't be discouraged when he has to show you where you are wrong. For when he punishes you, . . . it proves you are really his child.' Let God train you, for he is doing what any loving father does for his children. For whoever heard of a son who was never corrected? If God doesn't punish you when you need it, as other fathers punish their sons, then it means that you aren't really God's son at all—that you don't really belong in his family. . . . God's correction is always right and for our best good, that we may share his holiness.'" So that severe shock which you brought on yourself may well be understood as your heavenly Father trying to get through to you, that you're on the wrong track. Realistically, and sympathetically, that same writer to the Hebrews adds, "Being punished isn't enjoyable while it is happening—it hurts! But afterwards we can see the results, a quiet growth in grace and character."[10]

You might well be saying to yourself, "Man alive, if the Christian life is so rough, why bother?" The non-Christian life is even rougher, and with no reasonable explanations or purposes behind *any* of the difficulties. But most important of all, the non-Christian misses out on the loving fellowship of God providing safety in the midst of his trials—not to mention his missing the power of God to show him where the smooth air is, or give him both the courage and patience to ride out the storm.

When that awful, chattering turbulence was slamming that airliner around I thought it would never end . . . but it finally did, much to my relief!

25

Time slows down when trouble strikes, but Paul reminds us, "These troubles and sufferings of ours are, after all, quite small and won't last very long. Yet this short time of distress will result in God's richest blessing upon us forever and ever! So we do not look at what we can see right now, the troubles all around us, but we look forward to the joys in heaven which we have not yet seen. The troubles will soon be over, but the joys to come will last forever."[11]

Jesus said, "These things I have spoken unto you, that in me ye might have peace. In the world ye shall have tribulations but be of good cheer; I have overcome the world."[12]

"Fasten your seat belts, please!" If you keep that warning in plane view, you'll never be caught off your guard as you make good your flight path through this turbulent world.

Of course, there is the matter of your final destination to consider. You have considered it, haven't you?

Notes

1. Psalm 34:19, *The Living Bible*
2. Luke 13:1-5, *TLB*
3. Romans 8:28, *King James Version*
4. II Corinthians 1:8, *TLB*
5. I Peter 1:6,7, *TLB*
6. John 17:15,16, *TLB*
7. I John 1:8,10, *TLB*
8. Galatians 5:17, *TLB*
9. Hebrews 12:5-10, *TLB*
10. Hebrews 12:11, *TLB*
11. II Corinthians 4:17,18, *TLB*
12. John 16:33, *KJV*

The Flight Plan

CHAPTER 3

"Have you closed out your flight plan?" This sign confronted us as we drove out of the airport of a small city in western Canada. I read the words out loud. The mayor, our host for the sight-seeing flight just completed, admitted, "We didn't even file a flight plan!"

"Mr. Mayor," I said, "that's the problem of the whole human race. So few of us even file a flight plan for our lives. No really good pilot would dream of taking a trip of any distance without first deciding on his destination, carefully planning every detail of his journey, and then filing a flight plan with the authorities to help protect himself against any unforeseen misfortune that could over-take him en route. Yet most people take the journey of life—eventually into death—without the foggiest notion of their destination or how to cope with the dangers along the way."

One purpose of a flight plan is to remind the pilot that flying can be hazardous if he doesn't face squarely all the potential difficulties en route and make adequate provision for them. Is the terrain over which he must fly mountainous? Then he must plan to fly high enough to miss the highest peak, by a generous margin. Does his plane have enough fuel on board to reach his goal, with a surplus to allow for the unexpected? A head wind can reduce his speed over the ground, increase his fuel consumption and delay his arrival, or perhaps even keep him from ever reaching his destination. What about other aircraft? Where are they? Is there danger of collision with them? Perhaps one of the greatest hazards on the way is the weather. What is it like? Filing a flight plan forces a pilot to think, investigate and plan for any eventuality.

Living is hazardous, too! All of us finally run out of fuel and have to put down somewhere. Many of us spend our lives wondering if we have headed in the right direction. At best, most people have defined goals in life vaguely. Rarely does a person stop to think, "Where am I going? Why? How am I going to get there? What are the dangers en route? What's the purpose for my life anyway?" In filling out the destination for your life's flight plan, what will you write? In honesty, most of us would simply have to write, "the grave." Such a bleak prospect empties life of any enduring meaning. But futility is not God's will for your life or mine.

The Bible says, "For we all must die and are then like water spilled on the earth which cannot be recovered. . . . God, however, does not sweep away life, but rather takes measures so as not to keep the banished away from Himself."[1]

Some may have planned goals, such as success, prestige, money, love, pleasure, power, security and the like; but the lack of any sure knowledge of an ultimate destination hangs over us like a specter, casting a dark shadow over any lasting sense of fulfillment which achievement might bring. A few who have "arrived" at one or more of these goals, have discovered that the very nature of human existence demands that even before they fully enjoy the "arrival," they must move on. Such is the plight of those who arrive at the top of their profession—only to discover that the goal, which held out such promise of reward actually is less in realization than it was in anticipation. Indeed, arrival can even become their slave master. Having attained their goal in life they discover they must fight to maintain it, then are forced to push on whether they want to or not.

Almost always the struggle to "arrive" brings greater happiness than the actual achievement of these insufficient goals. "Arrival" brings back the nagging question, "Where do I go from here?"

Many young people, observing their elders' basic unhappiness after achieving lofty goals, decide there is no point in planning. Why not just drift along and live for the day? "Life has no meaning, and pleasure is the only reason for human existence," is their song. Hollywood in particular, and show business in general, have provided most of the heroes and heroines for youth. The frequent spectacle of professional success, coupled with personal

31

failure, has had its impact. The same pattern is reflected with alarming frequency in the main street of every town and city, as the divorce rate continues to soar, crime and corruption flourish; loveless homes abound and the purposeless, treadmill existence of the average citizen is observed with shrewd and critical eye by the youth of our land. Is it any wonder they are desperate in their search for more vital meaning in their lives?

As one student leader put it, "At the heart of the students' problem is their lack of meaning for living." Another echoed his sentiments: "This is the real crisis of the campus. Students have goals but no purpose. Students have plans but no conviction that they are proceeding in the right direction. Students have aspirations, but also frustration. They even have causes; yet their lives are meaningless."[2]

Each of us has a pretty good set of plans for what we think will make us happy. Why is it that even the loftiest human goals fail to yield what they promise? Basically, it is because God has devised the only perfect flight plan for our individual lives. Anything short of our discovering and executing His plan for us, generates frustration and empties the best accomplishments of their sense of complete fulfillment. Our plans are not necessarily evil—indeed they may even be good by the world's standards—but they are just not the ones designed to effect our greatest good.

Does God have a perfect plan for your flight through this world? The Bible answers with an emphatic "Yes."

"For I know the plans I have for you, says the

Lord. They are plans for good and not for evil, to give you a future and a hope."

"You will show me the path of life!" exults the believer who wrote Psalm 16:11. Again, the Psalmist cries, "You chart the path ahead of me, and tell me where to stop and rest. Every moment, you know where I am. You know what I am going to say before I say it. You both precede and follow me, and place your hand of blessing on my head. This is too glorious, too wonderful to believe! I can never be lost to your Spirit! I can never get away from my God! If I go up to heaven, you are there; if I go down to the place of the dead, you are there. If I ride the morning winds to the farthest oceans, even there your hand will guide me, your strength will support me."[4]

As if that were not enough to tell us that God does have a perfect plan, the Psalmist continues, "You saw me before I was born and scheduled each day of my life before I began to breathe. Every day was recorded in your Book! How precious it is, Lord, to realize that you are thinking about me constantly! I can't even count how many times a day your thoughts turn towards me! And when I waken in the morning, you are still thinking of me!"[5]

If, then, God has such a detailed flight plan for each person's life, why do so few people find it? The answer is so simple! We humans sincerely believe that we know better than God does what will make us happy, both in personal conduct and lifetime vocation. We develop tastes and desires; we have needs and ambitions; and we plan every possible way we can to satisfy every taste, desire, need and ambition. That these go contrary to God's standard of right and wrong is of little importance to us, because we really think we know best! The man or woman who violates the seventh commandment (or any of the ten) is declaring that he knows better than the God who made him what is going to make him happy.

This has been the problem from the beginning, *our insistence!* It is stunning how clearly and simply the whole matter is presented in the book of Genesis. God revealed to Adam and Eve His perfect plan for their happiness and fulfillment. They determined that they knew better than He did what would make them happy. The way of independence beckoned and they took it. Choosing their plan instead of His, they alienated themselves from the only Source of meaning for their lives.

Every individual born on the face of this earth exercises the same option, at one point or another in his or her life. Perhaps you say, "How do I *know* what God wants for me? I'd be happy to do the will of God if only I knew what it was!" The Bible says clearly in Romans 2:14 that God has written His will in *every* human heart in the form of the Ten Commandments. "Man," you say, "what's that got to do with where I'm headed in life or what I do in life?" The answer is that it has everything to do with what you are as a person. And what you *are* surely determines what you ultimately do.

The first four commandments concern your attitude toward God; the last six, your attitude toward your neighbor and yourself. The first commandment demands that you put God first. That's the first step in His plan for your life. Right here is where we have all messed up. We think a better plan is to put self first—anything but God first! Sin is not so much "badness" as it is a declaration of independence from God's perfect "flight plan." Having declared ourselves wiser than God and rejected the first step in His plan, it is no wonder that everything else tends to foul up. It's like buttoning a sweater. When the first button is wrong, all the others end up wrong as well.

When we hate, lie, steal and lust, we are declaring our plan is better than His. When we commit adultery and desire what properly belongs to others, we are insisting on our way, not His. This is why "arrival" at even the highest levels of earthly success fails to fulfill, and demands that the life trip continue on its relentless search for an ever elusive purpose. This is what it means to be lost. To be lost in a plane is a panicky business. Even if the ground is in view when you're lost, if there are no landmarks familiar to the eye, bewilderment and fear result. To discover you're lost in life can bring about the same awful sense of panic.

One day not too long ago, my wife and I were flying out of the West Virginia mountains. The weather was what the British would call "vile." The little single-engine airplane in which we were traveling was not overloaded with navigational equipment. We were on visual flight rules, which means that we were making our navigation on the basis of the landmarks that we could discern on the ground. Poor visibility and clouds that came down to the mountain tops necessitated some very quick changes of course. With his map on his knee, the pilot was busily peering toward the ground as I was flying the plane. There were some anxious moments for all of us until he finally sighed with relief and pointed to a small town. "Three bridges across the river. That's a grand landmark. Now I know exactly where we are!" he said.

In your life's journey can you say, "I know exactly where I am"? Can you add with equal certainty that you're the sort of person God wants you to be, and doing the life's work which He created you to do?

Our individual decisions to follow our own plans —rather than God's great plan for our lives—are what cause us to get lost. But Jesus Christ is God's great North Star of human navigation. When we reject His plan for our lives, we're cut loose from the only never-shifting point of reference in human experience upon which we can rely. Small wonder we get lost!

Too proud to ask for help? An air traffic control official of the Federal Aviation Agency indicated, in a recent letter, that most of the pilots who lost their way and crashed, might have been saved had they only admitted early enough to themselves that they were lost and appealed by radio for help. The Bible says, "Pride goes before a destruction."[6] It could just as well read, "Pride goes before a crash."

There are rare moments of truth that all of us have experienced, when death stalks a loved one, or we've had a close call, or some shattering disappointment. Then we know, deep in our hearts, that we have no never-changing point of reference to guide our lives; only a proud unwillingness to admit that the essential nature of our "lost" condition deludes us into thinking that we can make it without calling for help.

Many of us drift through life with no flight plan and no destination. We have long since lost any solid unchanging point of reference. Life has no purpose, yet pride keeps us from admitting that we are lost. All it takes to be found is for you to call out to God. You have His Word for it. "You will find me when you seek me, if you look for me in earnest."[7] "Call to Me and I will answer you and reveal to you great and mighty things which you do not know."[8]

Just be sure you call on the right frequency.

Notes

1. II Samuel 14:14, *The New Berkeley Version in Modern English.*
2. James R. Hiskey, former All-American Golfer, 1958, *Christianity Today.*
3. Jeremiah 29:11, *The Living Bible*
4. Psalm 139:3-10, *TLB*
5. Psalm 139:15-18, *TLB*
6. Proverbs 16:18, *TLB*
7. Jeremiah 29:13, *TLB*
8. Jeremiah 33:3, *Berkeley*

The Right Frequency

CHAPTER 4

Even the pilot who is admitting he's lost can open up on the radio and yell his head off for help with no result, if he's tuned to the wrong frequency. A radio is a narrow-minded instrument. It must be tuned in right or it won't function. To call on a frequency where no one is listening is an exercise in fearsome futility. A call to God must also be on the right frequency. Jesus said, "The Son of man is come to seek and to save that which was lost." Again, He said, "I am the way, the truth, and the life: no man cometh unto the Father, but by me." God is always sending and receiving signals in the person of Jesus Christ.

After the strain of a combat flight over Okinawa (World War II), what a comfort it was to tune in on the one signal which brought us home to the aircraft carrier. There was only one place on the dial to get that signal. With gas running low, daylight running out and little idea of where the ship was,

you can be sure that we didn't sit up there and argue about how narrow-minded it was to be able to get homing-help at one little spot on the dial. We knew our situation and tuned in on the only help available—the ship that sent the signal drew us home to the safety of its deck.

It is bad to be lost and not admit it. It is worse to be lost and not know it. Surely an honest look at the world and the national scene is enough to assure us that we are off the track somewhere. We never add up to more as a nation than the sum of what we are as individuals. Today's situation is a corporate symptom of individual disease. We keep hoping for public blessing, while being unwilling to pay the price of private, personal virtue. We've lost our way as a nation because we've lost God's way in our individual lives.

The person who sees he has lost his way in life, admits it, and knows the peril of his situation, is not about to debate the exclusive claims of Jesus Christ. He hears the loving words of Jesus' invitation, "Come unto me, all ye that labour and are heavy laden, and I will give you rest."³ He tunes into this eternal homing-help by faith, and hears the signal of Christ, "I am the door: by me if any man enter in, he shall be saved."⁴ That is, he shall be made safe from the consequences of his rebellion against God's perfect flight plan for him. Once he has surrendered to the idea that God's plan is better than his, and contact with the living God has been established, he will continue to get his homing signals from the Lord. Continuous guidance in the airways of safety will be his.

Late one afternoon as the sun was setting, I took off in a single-engine light plane from the airport in Nassau in the Bahamas, to make the 150-mile over-water return flight to Miami, Florida. As I climbed in a westerly direction, I consulted my map of the area. It told me that homing signals were being sent from a V.O.R. (visual omni range) station located in Biscayne Bay, just off the island of Key Biscayne. I could either believe what the map told me and tune to the listed radio frequency, or just muddle along and take my chances on dead reckoning ("dead reckoning" is a way of reckoning a course which has left a lot of people dead). A small mistake in heading, plus an increase in the cross wind from the north, might cause me to miss the main-land, the Florida Keys, and end up wandering around the Gulf of Mexico.

I tuned my radio to the exact spot on the dial and turned up the volume. I did this by faith! I had no proof that anyone was over there sending signals. The sun had disappeared and darkness was deepen-ing when I heard those first faint signals. I had acted by faith in what the map said and now I had experienced the signals that guided me to the safety of home. Later on, the lights of Miami brimmed over the black horizon providing a reassuring sight. As thrilling as flying is, it is always a good feeling to land safely.

The Bible is God's map for every life. It says that saving signals are always reaching out to us in the person of Jesus Christ. It says, "Salvation that comes from trusting Christ . . . is already within easy reach of each of us; in fact, it is as near as our own hearts and mouths. For if you tell others with your own mouth that Jesus Christ is your Lord, and believe in your own heart that God has raised him from the dead, you will be saved. For it is by believing in his heart that a man becomes right with God; and with his mouth he tells others of his faith, confirming his salvation. . . . Anyone who calls on the name of the Lord will be saved."[5]

God's map, the Bible, on one point of its dial says, "There is salvation in no one else! Under all heaven there is no other name for men to call upon to save them."[6] You can speculate forever about whether or not the "map" is telling the truth, but it is only when you act on what it requires that you will ever know for sure. The signals may be weak at first, but keep listening; obey them, and they will lead you home. Jesus said, "If any of you really determines to do God's will, then you will certainly know whether my teaching is from God or is merely my own."[7]

"You know these things—now do them!"[8] That is the path of blessing.

One of the comforting safety features of modern-day commercial air travel is the passengers' knowledge that the pilot is in constant communication with air traffic control personnel on the ground, to obtain their assistance and guidance.

Constant communication with God for the same purpose is the exciting prospect for the person who is committed to following God's flight plan for his life. God will always be sending His message of love and guidance through the Bible to the believer who approaches it with faith. The communication is

44

two ways. God invites us to respond. We call this response prayer. Prayer is talking to God as you would to the best friend you ever had. No special language is required (such as thee, thy, thine, didst, wast, shouldest, etc.), and no special posture is needed either. All that is required is a humble heart, mustard-seed faith, and a growing idea that His way is the best and only way.

The purpose of this two-way communication is twofold. God is interested in what we are, and He is interested in what we do. His priorities are in that order. He wants to change our way of *thinking*, *feeling* and *willing*. In short He wants to make us brand-new people, changed by His Holy Spirit at work inside us. This internal change comes as we begin to obey the communications which He relays through His Word and our prayer. The change on the inside then begins to *show* itself in our outward attitudes and actions. The person who really wants to become the kind of man that God wants him to be, will also begin to sense the unfolding of God's perfect flight plan for his life. This takes time—but it's worth it to discover why God made you, and to know for certain that He loves you, forgives you, and is beginning to reveal to you His perfect plan for your life.

Just as the pilot consults his map to chart his course and be alerted to dangers, the believer consults God's map to chart his course through life. No map can cover every eventuality or conceivable circumstance that may confront the pilot. There are simply too many variables. To cover these he must get his information somewhere else.

The Bible is a reliable map for life, but there are numerous variables that can conjure up situations not covered specifically in the Bible. What a joy to communicate with God about these situations and seek His solutions. You have the promise of His Word that He will answer and guide you: "I will instruct you (says the Lord) and guide you along the best pathway for your life; I will advise you and watch your progress."[9]

In life almost no problems, even the simple ones, can be resolved among men if communication breaks down. Among other reasons, Jesus Christ came to this earth in order to reestablish continual communication between men and God, and among human beings. Dial your heart to the person of Jesus Christ and, now, listen again to the invitation of God, "Call to Me and I will answer you and reveal to you great and mighty things which you do not know."[10] But, to know for sure that *this is your signal, you must act! Now, call!!!*

Notes

1. Luke 19:10, *King James Version*
2. John 14:6, *KJV*
3. Matthew 11:28, *KJV*
4. John 10:9, *KJV*
5. Romans 10:8-10,13, *The Living Bible*
6. Acts 4:12, *TLB*
7. John 7:17, *TLB*
8. John 13:17, *TLB*
9. Psalm 32:8, *TLB*
10. Jeremiah 33:3, *The New Berkeley Version in Modern English*
11. Deuteronomy 4:29-31, *Berkeley*

The Simulator

CHAPTER 5

Some years ago, while in England, I was invited to speak to a gathering of workers at a large English aircraft factory. After the meeting an aeronautical engineer took my wife and me on a tour of the factory which made the three-jet transport named the Trident. He showed us a room loaded with a remarkable collection of computers and electronic devices, linked together with a completely instrumented airliner cockpit. "This," he said, "is the flight simulator for the Trident. Our test pilots 'flew' this *before* we made the first plane."

Into this particular model they had fed all the data concerning the Trident *before they ever built it*. The computers took this detailed information about the "plane-to-be" and translated it into a simulation of the flight characteristics. The controls of that earthbound cockpit responded just as they would in a real airplane in flight. Test pilots could

sit in the planeless cockpit and know how the Trident would react to a variety of situations. Before them was even a screen that simulated a cockpit view of a lighted runway being approached by the imaginary plane they were flying.

The engineers told us that due to what they and the test pilots learned from the simulator, three major and numerous minor changes were made in the Trident's design. Who knows how many lives were saved as a result of their being able to fly this plane *before* it had ever been built.

Some time later, through the kindness of a United States Air Force major, I was permitted to fly a simulator programmed for one of the Phantom F4-C Fighters. I distinguished myself by becoming the only person to crash one of these fighters on take-off and landing, and all in the same flight. When this happened, I laughed with Navy embarrassment. "This is a cheap way to have crack-ups without loss of men or machines!" I said. The major responded, "That's the whole purpose of the simulator! You let your mistakes cause your crashes here, rather than in the plane itself!"

Three or four weeks after our tour of the English factory, we were stunned to read in a London paper that one of the Tridents had crashed while on a test flight. Ground observers indicated that the huge plane had come spinning almost straight down, rotating like a seed from a maple tree! This sounded as though the plane had gone into a dreaded flat spin. Preliminary investigations suggested that nothing had gone wrong with the plane either structurally or mechanically. The investigators could only conclude that the crash had been caused by pilot error.

In spite of all the advantages that the simulator had provided to both designers and pilots, human error had intruded itself at agonizing cost. What lesson had the simulator tried to teach in advance that somehow had been missed? But, without the simulator how much higher would have been the price in men and machines?

When I first saw the airplane simulator operate, it occurred to me: "The Bible is God's great *life simulator*. Its pages have been programmed with the real historic lives of ordinary human beings who have made about every conceivable blunder possible for men to make. It not only shows the dismal plight of a man without God, but also the exciting possibilities of a man with God." About itself the Bible says, "All those writings of long ago were written for our instruction, so that through the patience and encouragement of the Scriptures we might have hope."[1] In seeing both the mistakes and their consequences in the lives of others, we can by God's grace, set our course to avoid both. Let's look at some of the real lives programmed into the Bible.

Take Esau for instance. Here was a man of tremendous potential. Yet in a moment's lapse, he could give way to an impatient bodily appetite and swap his birthright for a bowl of beans. Sure, he had help from a deceitful brother; but the Bible indicates that Esau never recovered from this fouled-up sense of values. We can learn from that momentary lapse the possible long-range consequences of similar failures in our own lives.

I believe it was Lord Acton who said, "Power tends to corrupt and absolute power corrupts absolutely."' But, long before he said it, the life of King Saul recorded the sad deterioration of a man of humble beginnings ending up with too much power. Unwilling to submit to the authority and direction of the King of heaven, his unrepentant life came to a tragic conclusion. Before his death he even descended to the appalling depths of witchcraft and communication with the dead. Granted that none of us has ever had his kind of power, but how do we use or misuse the power we do have? At work? At home? Saul wanted the advantages of a religion which could give him some sort of assurance for his future, without making any moral demands on his present personal life. This is why he inevitably ended up looking for answers in the occult. Today's obsession with astrology, seances, witchcraft and the occult has its origins in the same desire—a religion without moral demands! Programmed into the pages of this ancient book, the Bible, are relevant warnings that are startling in their contemporary applications. We can vicariously fly Saul's crash course in the great life Simulator and then resolve that by God's grace we'll avoid that kind of crash in our own lives.

Remember David? The shepherd boy who became king of Israel? It is hard to imagine a more remarkable combination of talents and human qualities. He had it all: brave and aggressive, tender and compassionate, a military genius, a literary giant, superb musician, a great leader of men. Yet during an idle moment, a casual stroll in his roof garden started a chain of events that led to adultery, an illegitimate pregnancy, and, finally, an arranged murder. It was during this stroll that he saw Bathsheba, his neighbor's wife, bathing. Her exceptional beauty was such a stimulus to David that he sent for her; and, in spite of the fact that her husband was off fighting David's war, she willingly engaged in sex with him on the first meeting. The resultant pregnancy pushed David into a desperate and despicable effort to cover up his sin by recalling Bathsheba's husband from the front. When he wouldn't go home to his wife, David ordered him back into the war, with treacherous instructions to his commanders to put him in the hottest part of the fight (and then contriving a withdrawal), assuring his death.

One can almost move step by step with David's mental process. First the overwhelming visual stimulus, then the mental fantasy of the exciting details of sex with Bathsheba, then the move to do what he knew was wrong, then the need to cover up which led to a cowardly murder.

Only the prophet Nathan's confrontation of David with the awfulness of what he had done, trapping him in his own condemnation, brought from him heartbroken repentance and confession. Psalm 51 is David's cry to God for forgiveness. From this we see that David knew where the problem originated. He pinpointed his (and our) problem when he prayed, "Create in me a new, clean heart, O God, filled with clean thoughts and right desires."' In David we see the potential for evil in the best and most talented of us.

53

The Bible says, "These experiences came to them as a lesson for us and were written as a warning to us, on whom the end of the age has come. Therefore, let him who feels sure of standing firm, beware of falling." The prophet Isaiah cried out to the people of his day, "Won't even one of you apply these lessons from the past and see the ruin that awaits you up ahead?"[5]

On the positive side the Bible shows man's great potential when he's ready to let God direct his life, regardless of the cost. For instance, Daniel risked his life to live God's way while a captive in a foreign land. God delivered him from lions, political intrigue, the seducing influences of a pagan court, and elevated him to an incredible position of power that finally brought the heathen king to acknowledge Daniel's God as the only God.

The pinnacle of instruction in God's Simulator is when He programmed Himself into the Person of Jesus of Nazareth. As we look at Him, we discover the attitude of God toward the blunders of man, and the actions of God to remedy those blunders. The Bible says, "For in Christ there is all of God in a human body."[6] His dealings with men and women in their failures is what brings that "steadying and comforting of the Scriptures" to the reader who seriously takes to heart His message. When Jesus died our death and took our hell on the cross, His act demonstrated His forgiveness and love.

When impulsive Peter is reinstated by Jesus after his shameful triple failures, we reason that a similar penitence on our part will bring a similar response from God.

The woman taken in the act of adultery is forgiven by Jesus, and the self-righteous stuffed shirts who flung her at His feet are withered by His words. We reason that a confession by us that He is Lord and Saviour will bring a similar response of the loving forgiveness of God.

The philosopher, Kierkegaard, once wrote, "We live frontwards, but we learn backwards!" He probably meant we learn from looking back! In the Bible we learn not only by looking back at the mistakes and failures of others, but from their victories through the use of God's ever available enabling power. By looking back into the face of Jesus we discover what God is like right now.

As a flight simulator can tell us the characteristic reactions of an airplane to a variety of situations, so the Bible is telling what life is like, what we are like, and most of all what God is like—how we react *and He acts*. It lets us see the tragedy of moral smashups in individual lives and nations. It shows us that in the affairs of men, unbelief always corrupts behavior. In observing these things in God's great Simulator and heeding the direction it gives, we avoid the inevitable crashes that human sin always brings. Vicariously experiencing both the sin and its tragic consequence, the forgiveness and the staggering patience of the God of love, we then ask Him to work in the present reality of our own lives.

A pilot who does all his flying in the simulator doesn't really ever fly; and, similarly many church people have assimilated an academic philosophy as a substitute for a dynamic experience with Jesus. They are like an aeronautical engineer who has never been off the ground—who knows all the intricate theories of aerodynamics, planes and flying, yet who has never known the exhilarating thrill of breaking free from the earth's surface to explore the heavenly home of the stars. The ultimate intention of God's Simulator—the Bible—is that you request God to program His Son into your heart and life, so that you might experience in personal reality what you know vicariously from the Simulator. God's Holy Spirit will do this for you right now! All you have to do is ask Him in. The Lord of Peter, James, John and Paul must become your Lord—the God of Abraham, David and Daniel wants to become the living God in your life today! ". . . For the Father is looking for such as His worshipers."[7] *"So you have everything when you have Christ, and you are filled with God through your union with Christ. He is the highest Ruler, with authority over every other power."*[8]

Notes

1. Romans 15:4, *The New Berkeley Version in Modern English*
2. For reference please consult *The Oxford Dictionary of Quotations*, 2nd Edition, p. 1, and *Jesus Power*, by Sherwood Eliot Wirt, p. 8, with note, p. 115.
3. Psalm 51:10, *The Living Bible*
4. I Corinthians 10:11,12, *Berkeley*
5. Isaiah 42:23, *TLB*
6. Colossians 2:9, *TLB*
7. John 4:23, *Berkeley*
8. Colossians 2:10, *TLB*

An Ill Wind

CHAPTER 6

A pilot taxies his small single-engine plane to the end of the runway at Miami International Airport. The tower clears him for take-off. He applies full power, lifts smoothly off, and heads for Kennedy Airport in New York some 1060 miles away. The weather is perfect. The sun is shining. Having consulted a reliable map he knows the precise direction he must fly to reach New York. He banks his plane until the compass shows he's exactly on course, levels his wings and continues to climb. Arriving at his planned altitude for the flight, he adjusts his throttle and propeller pitch so that his air speed is 142 miles-per-hour. At this rate, he'll reach his destination in a little over seven and one-half hours and still have enough fuel on board for over two hours' extra flying time as a safety factor.*

Over Palm Beach the coast of Florida begins to

*Note: Navigation problem figured using a single-engine Cessna 210 Centurion aircraft, at 10,000 feet, using economy range.

slip away under the left wing. The most direct route takes him far enough over the Atlantic, to lose sight of land. The engine sounds healthy—everything is perfect. The sun sets. Rose-colored sky fades into gray, then into velvet black. The air is smooth as wet glass. The night is beautiful. Stars are everywhere. He settles in his seat for a comfortable flight.

Sometime later he begins to look for the eastern shore of North Carolina. Instead he finds an unexpected cover of clouds shrouding the earth. No matter, he has held perfectly to his course. The clouds continue to obscure the coast line. Time passes.

Now, according to his reckoning, Atlantic City should be directly beneath him. A few more minutes on course and he peers out into the darkness. Up ahead the cloud cover seems to end—it does end—he sighs with relief! But the relief is short-lived.

The lights! Where are the lights from all the cities along the North Jersey shore? From here he ought to be able to see the New York City night sky dramatically aglow. He swivels his head in all directions! No lights anywhere—not even a faint glimmer. His heart begins to pound—his mouth is dry—his hands are clammy. The deep darkness beneath him can only be water—the Atlantic Ocean. Fighting panic, his eyes search the western sky for some trace of light. There is none. With water beneath him, land has to lie to the west—but how far west? He has two hours and fifty-four minutes of fuel remaining. Will it be enough?

The answer is "No!" Our mythical pilot is 387 miles at sea to the east of Kennedy Airport. You might well ask, "If he stayed on course the whole way, how could he end up so far from his destination, and without any hope of arriving?"

Suppose I answered you, "An unseen but powerful force pushed him slowly out to sea with such subtlety that he was unaware of the mortal danger until it was too late." It sounds mysterious and sinister, doesn't it? But suppose I simply state, "A 45-mile-per-hour wind from the west blew him out to sea." It doesn't make it any less deadly, does it?

I have always found it somewhat amazing that anyone, especially a flyer, could ever say, "I only believe in what I can see!" No one has ever seen the wind. We find it easy to believe in the wind because we can observe the effect of it. No one has ever seen the air; but we find it easy to believe in the air because every human being's life is maintained by his moment-by-moment intake of the air he cannot see. If we honestly refuse to believe in what we cannot see then we must stop breathing Only a stupid pilot would ignore the influence of the wind simply because he cannot see it.

To ignore even a slight cross wind at the beginning of a flight can mean disaster at the end. The small mistake at the outset grows with every mile traveled. How fatal it can be to ignore the final influence of even a slight initial error.

All of us have heard the saying, "Tis an ill wind that blows no man to good!"[1] The Bible insists that there is an ill wind that blows no man to good. A cursory glance at our history books or the daily newspapers confirms this in a frightening way. An honest analysis of our own personal lives offers an unnerving corroboration. We don't drift toward God and good, but rather toward evil and the Devil. An unseen but powerful force is subtly pushing us off the straight and narrow course. The small deviation at the commencement of life finally leaves us desperately far off the mark at the end of life. An ill wind of hurricane force might alarm us to take remedial steps, but balmy breezes of evil influence ease us off course in a most delightful way. We rarely remember how it happened, or when.

Particularly is it so in this day and age when traditional moral guidelines are being blown away by permissiveness. We drift without even realizing it. How could it be otherwise when "entertainment" always seems to include murder, immorality and mayhem? How could it be otherwise when religious leaders are rejecting the standards of the Ten Commandments by calling them the invention of a man named Moses, instead of the revelation of the will of a holy God? Jeremiah's question to this day fits our situation, "Were they embarrassed when they committed abominations? No, they were not at all embarrassed; they did not even know how to blush; therefore they shall fall among the fallen; during the time that I punish them, they shall be overthrown, says the Lord."[2]

But not only are those in danger who participate in such wanton disregard of God's moral guidelines. We who deplore these immoral actions in others quite often are set adrift ourselves by such conduct. This subtle process of moral drift was well described by Alexander Pope in his "Essay on Man," when he said,

> "Vice is a monster of so frightful mien,
> As to be hated needs but to be seen;
> Yet seen too oft, familiar with her face,
> We first endure, then pity, then embrace."[3]

In this way all of us are subject to the ill winds of our day.

The parallel between the wind blowing a plane off course and evil blowing a man's life off course is not as far-fetched as one might think. "The Hebrew word *ruach* means either 'wind' or 'breath' or 'spirit', according to context."[4] The Bible speaks of evil spirits (winds) as a reality. The presence of powerful evil influences in our lives confirms this truth. Moreover, the Bible says of this world system that it is "controlled by the ruler of the kingdom of the air, the spirit of the one now working in disobedient people."[5]

For those who might find this too simple an explanation for the presence of evil influences in this world, I suggest this consideration: for all of man's advances in scientific technology, psychiatry, social science, medicine, economics and general education —there yet remains a power of evil so abrasive in the affairs of men that the whole world grinds toward a human explosion of evil so vast and catastrophic that it boggles the mind to contemplate. There is an ill wind (spirit) at work in this world that blows no man to good.

A pilot has four basic steps to take in order to keep from being blown off course.

1. He must accept the reality of the wind as a

danger in spite of the fact that he cannot see it.

2. He must determine the direction from which it comes and its force.

3. He must correct his course by turning his plane into the wind sufficiently to make good his intended course over the earth's surface.

4. He must be ever alert to the need for further possible course corrections, because a change in wind direction, or wind force, or both, demands a new course.

So, also, a man must accept the reality of the ill wind in life as a grave danger in spite of the fact that he cannot see "it," only its effects. J. S. Whale, the Cambridge scholar, wrote a book in 1936 entitled, *The Christian Answer to the Problem of Evil.* In 1957 I heard him say, "I really ought to rewrite the book! Now I'd have a lot more to say about the Devil!" The years of experiencing life in this world had taught him the grim reality of evil.

My friend, Calvin Thielman, pressed for his reasons for believing in a personal devil, answered, "I believe in a personal devil because the Bible says so, and because I've done business with him!"

The Bible says we humans naturally tend to be, ". . . blown about by every shifting wind of the teaching of deceitful men, who lead others to error by the tricks they invent."⁶ If we are to stop being blown about, we need to accept as a reality the presence of evil in this world, not only objective to us but subjectively within us.

Next, we need to discover the direction from which the evil comes and face it even if it means acknowledging that the greatest source is within ourselves.

Anything that takes us away from God and good should be suspect. To gauge the force of evil's effect upon us, we simply have to compare our lives to the life of Jesus Christ. He kept the Ten Commandments so perfectly that even His worst enemies could not convict Him of sin. Jesus' life is what the Ten Commandments look like when lived out in day-to-day personal and corporate relationships. Therefore, His conduct represents the perfect God-pleasing course through life. It is when we try to obey the Bible and "follow His steps" that we see clearly how far away from His course of conduct we actually are. Only Jesus Christ indwelling a man can impart to him the ability and direction to make a true track through this windy world.

Mature Christians all testify that the provisions they made for both the force and direction of the ill wind of yesterday must be altered for today's temptations. The Devil is the arch deceiver and once he sees we have made the necessary corrections for certain of his temptations, he changes the force and direction of his ill wind. In the beginning of a Christian's life, he is struggling to keep from being blown constantly off course into the sins of the flesh. When the presence of Christ gives him victory here (and he's making good progress on a true course), all the Devil then has to do is stop that ill wind from blowing and our hero is in danger of flying off into the sin of smug self-righteousness which, again, brings him on the opposite side of his God-given track (see illustration).

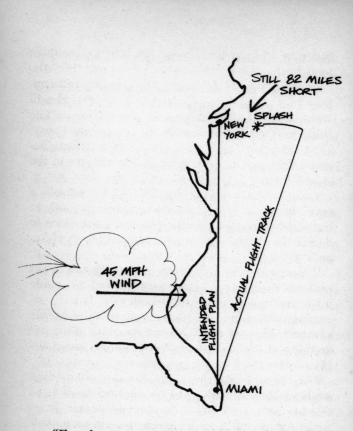

"For this purpose the Son of God appeared, to destroy the works of the devil."⁸ That's good news for those of us who are so easily taken off course by the ill wind that blows no man to good. The next verse goes on to tell how Christ accomplishes this. "The person who has been born into God's family does not make a practice of sinning, because now God's life is in him; so he can't keep on sinning, for this new life has been born into him and controls him—he has been *born again*."⁹ This new life, the very life of God, is born into the believer and controls him. This is how Jesus Christ defeats the ill wind from any direction and at any force. The Bible says to the believer in a very personal way, "You are from God . . . and have defeated them, because the One in you is greater than the one in the world."¹⁰

Only as Jesus Christ by His Spirit controls a man's life on a daily basis, can he hope to be able to make the constantly changing course corrections to defeat the ever changing patterns and forces of Satan's ill wind.

The experienced pilot reading these words might well say to himself, "I cannot conceive of a sensible pilot, making a trip of this length and danger, not communicating at regular intervals with available authorities for weather information, or not using everything at his disposal to determine his position." My response is, "Sir, you have just made my point!"

Why would anyone fail to do the same thing while making his trip through the uncertainties of this life into the dark destination of death? Jesus said, "Ask, and it shall be given you; seek, and you shall find; knock, and it shall be opened unto you."¹¹ Isn't it equally absurd not to take advantage of His offer and ask Him for the latest words on winds aloft, as well as life-position checks in order that you might keep your ultimate destination in plane view?

So why not admit that Jeremiah is right when he said, "O Lord, I know it is not within the power of man to map his life and plan his course—so you correct me, Lord; but please be gentle. Don't do it in your anger, for I would die."[12] His (the Lord's) corrections will bring your true course into plane view.

Notes

1. John Heywood (1497-1580), *The Proverbs of John Heywood*, Part 2, chapter 9 (from *Familiar Quotations by John Bartlett*, published by Little, Brown, 1955).
2. Jeremiah 6:15, *The New Berkeley Version in Modern English*
3. Alexander Pope (1688-1744), "Essay on Man," epistle 2, line 217 (from *Familiar Quotations by John Bartlett*).
4. *Berkeley* (page 856, footnote to Ezekiel 37:9,10: "Then He said to me: Prophesy to the wind; prophesy, son of man, and say to the wind, Thus says the Lord God: Come from the four winds, O Spirit, and breathe upon these slain, that they may live. . . .").
5. Ephesians 2:2, *Berkeley*
6. Ephesians 4:14, *Today's English Version of the New Testament*
7. I Peter 2:21, *King James Version*
8. I John 3:8, *Berkeley*
9. I John 3:9, *The Living Bible*
10. I John 4:4, *Berkeley*
11. Matthew 7:7, *KJV*
12. Jeremiah 10:23,24, *TLB*

Vertigo

In World War II I was a Navy fighter pilot based on an aircraft carrier out in the Pacific. Most of the duty that I saw was around the island of Okinawa. The carrier division to which I was attached was engaged with the enemy for fifty-six consecutive days without relief.

On one particular day that we were launched, the clouds were literally scraping the top of the radar mast on the ship. The weather around Okinawa at this time of year was usually foul. Our division of four fighter planes rendezvoused just off the surface of the water, and then started off on what proved to be a four-hour flight in the clouds. I was in the second section of two planes, flying the "tail and Charlie" position. We were on instruments almost from the moment the flight leader pointed the nose of his plane upward and we followed him in close formation into the clouds. We were looking for a kami-

kaze plane that was circling our fleet. The Japanese suicide pilot probably was having as hard a time trying to find our fleet as we were about to have, trying to find him.

From the flagship, the radar operator directed us on one intercept course after another, hoping that somewhere in the clouds we'd find a cave-like clearing big enough to see for a half mile or more. Perhaps we could manage to cross paths with this kamikaze in the clearing. In following the radar's direction, we were involved in some rapid alterations of course and speed; sometimes right, or left, sometimes faster, sometimes slower, at times gaining altitude and at other times descending, always searching for the enemy. One hour went by. Two hours went by. The nerve-racking nature of close-formation flying the clouds without reference to sea or sky began to grind on my insides.

The radar operator called for a quick change of course and speed. The urgency of his tone was somewhat different from his other commands. In the radical maneuver that followed, the man upon whose wing I was flying didn't make the turn, and in an instant, the other two planes were out of sight and we were alone. My section leader quickly notified radar that we had lost the other two planes. They assured us that this was all right and they would give us separate instructions in order to intercept the suicide plane. We were given a course, altitude and speed to fly, and then for a time we received no more instructions from the ship.

After about fifteen minutes I began to have the feeling that somehow we were slowing down. I checked my air speed indicator and discovered we were losing speed. Quickly I checked the altimeter. It indicated we were gaining altitude and were in a very nose-high attitude. But the flagship hadn't told us to alter speed or altitude! I peered closely at the other pilot. He looked over, smiled and waved. He looked fine. Again I checked the air speed and realized that we were getting dangerously slow—so slow that collision between the two of us was imminent. I made a quick decision. Throwing on full power, I shot past the other plane and pumped the stick, indicating that he was now to follow me! Then I shoved over into straight and level flight, according to my instruments. I looked back at my buddy flying the other plane and saw that he had a completely bewildered look on his face.

(In spite of over another hour of searching, we never found the kamikaze and, fortunately, he never found the fleet. We never knew what happened to him.)

Later, after we had landed back on the carrier, my section leader reported to me that he had been under the impression that his airplane had been going straight and level at the time that I took over the lead of the section. He was unaware of the fact that he was climbing and slowing down so dangerously that, if he had continued in that way, he would have spun back into me and probably killed us both.

What he had was *vertigo*. A U.S. Naval aviation publication describes it: "Vertigo is an error or illusion of spacial orientation, an experience in which the pilot is confused about his relationship to the

73

earth or to other objects in the sky." In other words, a pilot with vertigo simply doesn't know which end is up. Pilots aren't the only victims of this condition. Birds can get vertigo. Ballet dancers get vertigo. Eskimos in kayaks get vertigo, too.

In spite of the fact that flight training warns pilots continually of the dangers of vertigo, scores of plane crashes, every year, are probably caused by it.

One of the things most feared by any pilot is to be in the clouds and become involved in a "graveyard spiral." That's when the pilot loses his sense of relationship to the earth, and the effort that he makes to put himself right compounds the error. Let me explain. Here is a man who looks at his instruments and sees that his air speed is building up alarmingly. He is in a nose-down attitude, but doesn't realize that one wing is also low. What would be his first reaction? He'd pull straight back on the stick. Well, what would that do? That would pull him into a tight spiral. The harder he pulls, the tighter the spiral. The result, if he keeps pulling back on the stick, is a continuing buildup of air speed and loss of altitude. The roar of the building air speed, the scream of the air past the canopy, the unwinding altimeter, and a grip of panic plus a good case of vertigo have killed hundreds, perhaps thousands, of pilots. The numbers are hard to estimate because the crashes are usually fatal.

A pilot being taught how to fly on instruments has this drummed into him: when you get into the clouds and lose visual reference to the ground, *forget everything you think, forget everything you feel. Concentrate on what those instruments tell you. Believe them and nothing else* and correct your airplane's flight according to what those instruments tell you rather than what your emotions or your reason tell you.

It is a confusing, frightening and bewildering experience to have both reason and feelings shouting that the plane's relationship to the ground is one thing, and to have the instruments report that the reverse is true. One must discipline himself to reject those insistent feelings in favor of the message of the instrument panel, and even then it's a struggle.

That's why (at least part of the reason) it comes as such a shock to us to consult God's instrument panel for our lives and have it tell us that we all have spiritual vertigo. The Bible says, "But your sins have separated you and your God; your iniquities have hidden His face from you."[1] Our sin separates us from God just like the clouds separate the pilot from the earth. "Therefore their way shall become to them as slippery places in the dark; they shall be thrust along and fall. . . ."[2]

Because our sin has separated us from a knowledge of God, we falsely assume that God has no knowledge of us, nor what we do. The Bible clearly indicates that God has a personal, detailed knowledge of us. When we have lost our reference point to the never changing God, everything else in life is out of kilter, and our best efforts at self-analysis and self-help will only serve to compound the initial error and worsen our situation.

The clouds of sin, anger, violence, war, famine and political oppression hide from us anything that seems stable or constant. Yet the eye of faith fastens on God's instrument panel, the Bible, giving us the capacity to penetrate those threatening clouds and revealing the never changing love of a God who calls out, "Come unto me, all ye that labour and are heavy laden, and I will give you rest."[3]

This same instrument panel that analyzes our situation provides our way out. The eye of faith that accepts God's analysis of our situation will discover God's remedy for that situation. Jesus Christ, the Son of God, can put us into a proper relationship with His Father, because He died the death (that we deserve) to drive away the cloud of our sin obscuring God. Salvation for a pilot with vertigo is not a matter of a certain feeling or reason, but faith in what his instruments tell him his condition is and what the remedy is. Faith in the finished work of Christ and a yielding to Him as Lord bring this sweet promise from the Word of God: "I have caused your transgressions to vanish like a cloud and your sins as a fog; return to Me, for I have redeemed you. Sing, O heavens, for the Lord has done it. . . ."[4]

"There is a way which seemeth right unto a man," we are told in the book of Proverbs, "but the end thereof are the ways of death."[5] There was a way that seemed right to my friend upon whose wing I was flying. He was flying that plane the best he knew how. He thought he was going straight and level, but the facts were completely contrary to what he felt and what he thought! He was ready to kill us both.

There are many ways that seem perfectly right in this life, many things that allure and seduce, but the Scripture says if they are contrary to the will of God, then the end thereof are the ways of death. The great tragedy of vertigo is that those that have it are rarely aware that they do have it, until it is too late. Nothing is more disastrous than to imagine we're going to make it to heaven some other way than by the cross of Jesus Christ. Jesus said, "No man cometh unto the Father, but by me."[6] Christ is the only way to be relieved of spiritual vertigo.

One of the typical ways, seemingly right, is to say, "God gave me a mind to think with, and I'm going by what my reason says is right!" Yet, God's instrument panel says that our minds have spiritual vertigo and that they have been blinded by sin. "If our gospel be hid, it is hid to them that are lost: in whom (Satan) hath blinded the minds of them which believe not."[7] Until we have received Christ and have established a proper relationship with our heavenly Father, we are groping helplessly through this life in the clouds of our own sin.

Instead of trusting in one's mind as the end-all and be-all, the Bible says, "Trust in the Lord with all thine heart; and lean not unto thine own understanding. In all thy ways acknowledge him, and he shall direct thy paths."[8] It is for this reason that the Word of God warns us not to depend solely on our minds. Life is larger than logic. The living of one day, or even one hour, so far transcends human logic that no man could adequately record all of the aspects of human existence for even so brief a time. (My flying friend was sincere, but he was wrong.)

Even though we live in a day when the chaos and bewilderment in institutions of higher learning

77

have caused man to have great doubt both about the final impact of education and the limits of human reason to solve our mounting problem, few have dared to voice similar doubt about the capacity of human feelings to be a deceptive and a lousy guide. How many parents have treacherously misguided their children by glibly saying, "Just follow what your heart tells you to do." In utter contrast to this, God's instrument panel warns, "He that trusteth in his own heart is a fool. . . ."[9]

Why does the Bible see the seat of the emotions as such an untrustworthy guide? Because, "The heart is deceitful above all things, and desperately wicked: who can know it?"[10] Modern day statistics about matters of the heart would certainly be on the Bible's side. Not merely the staggering divorce rate, but also the misery and unhappiness present in so many marriages, is what prompted a recent Associated Press dispatch to headline, "Happiness in Marriage Is an Oddity, Doctor Says!"[11]

Or you can look for advice to some "great intellect" or "hero"; only to discover in the process of time that he, too, is very human and that he, too, is infected with spiritual vertigo. This is one of the major reasons for disillusionment and cynicism in our day, because people discover that their human idols have feet of clay. This is what Jesus meant when He warned of the blind leading the blind and both ending up in the ditch. This is why God's instrument panel sharply warns about putting any other human being in that ultimate position that God alone can occupy. It says, "Cursed is the man who trusts in man and makes flesh his arm, whose

78

heart departs from the Lord.'"[12] But a brief verse later, the same divine instrument that tells us where help isn't, also tells us where help is. "Blessed is the man who trusts in the Lord and whose confidence is the Lord.'"[13]

In whom, then, can you trust? In God and in His sure Word.

The more experience a pilot has using his instruments in the clouds, the more he learns to trust what those instruments tell him in favor of what his feelings or his reason tell him. For almost twenty years now, I have been flying through this life, subordinating both feeling and reason in favor of the clear instruction of the Word of God. When, in following the Word of God, one discovers that this is the way, the truth and the life, confidence in that Word as a trustworthy instrument of guidance grows by leaps and bounds. Confirmation of the rightness of His guidance makes trust in Him grow.

It would be preposterous to expect someone uninstructed in how to use the instrument panel of an airplane, to step into that airplane, fly it and rely on the guidance of those instruments when he hasn't got a clue as to how they work. A man has to have knowledge, through instruction, in order to know how to use these instruments. So, also, a person needs an instructor to be able to understand the message of God's instrument panel, the Bible. The living Christ has promised to provide, precisely, such a One, when He said, ". . . But the Helper, the Holy Spirit, whom the Father will send in My name, He will teach you everything and will remind you of all that I have told you."[14]

Again, Jesus pointing to the necessity of His physical departure from this world, said, "However, I tell you the truth: My going is for your benefit; for if I do not leave, the Helper will not come to you; but if I go, then I will send Him to you. When the Spirit of Truth comes, however, He will guide you into all truth; for He will not speak on His own account but will say whatever He hears, and He will make known to you what is to take place."[15]

When the same Spirit that inspired the original Bible writers invades the Bible reader's heart, his mind becomes increasingly illuminated with instruction concerning the meaning of what he reads in the Word of God. That same Spirit, indwelling the hearts and minds of other believers, can likewise provide good counsel and instruction through other more mature people committed to the Lord Jesus Christ.

However, let us be honest and realistic. A bornagain, believing Christian is not completely removed from all possibility of recurring vertigo. As a matter of fact, as he is maturing, he learns how desperately he needs the instruction of the Word of God and the illumination of the Holy Spirit to keep him flying straight and level through a world that is clouded by sin. Even when his own life is right with God, the clouds of sin and confusion created by other lives in open rebellion against God are enough to provide such obscuring of the face of God that continuing vertigo is a real danger for the Christian.

But once a Christian really gets hold of this truth and lives his life every day with reliance upon

God's instrument panel and God's great Instructor, the Holy Spirit, he is assured that no amount of bewildering confusion can be fatal to him. One day every cloud will be gone and everything will be in plane view, even the face of God.

One might well ask, "Is the Christian's life then a cold and continuing denial of feeling and reason—a rigid following of signals from an impersonal panel of written gauges?" No indeed. The indwelling Holy Spirit is very real and very personal. Actually, this divine Instructor accompanies the Christian on every flight.

Notes

1. Isaiah 59:1,2, *The New Berkeley Version in Modern English*
2. Jeremiah 21:12, *Berkeley*
3. Matthew 11:28, *King James Version*
4. Isaiah 44:22,23, *Berkeley*
5. Proverbs 14:12, *KJV*
6. John 14:6, *KJV*
7. II Corinthians 4:3,4, *KJV*
8. Proverbs 3:5-6, *KJV*
9. Proverbs 28:26, *KJV*
10. Jeremiah 17:9, *TLB*
11. Associated Press dispatch, April 1967.
12. Jeremiah 17:5, *Berkeley*
13. Jeremiah 17:7, *Berkeley*
14. John 14:26, *Berkeley*
15. John 16:7,13, *Berkeley*

The Sensing Light

CHAPTER 8

It wasn't fear I felt as much as aloneness. The last
vestige of diffused light was rapidly fading, and the
little single-engined Cessna seemed even smaller
than usual in the cavernous space of the darkening
clouds. As the aircraft strained for more altitude
and slipped into the clouds, we were almost relieved to have the swirling mists replace the yawn-
ing space about us.

The three of us aboard the little craft had hardly
spoken a word since leaving a fueling stop just
southwest of Birmingham. There the pilot had indicated that the weather between us and Knoxville,
Tennessee, was such that we would have to file a
new flight plan, this time on instruments instead of
visual. Once aloft he was busy on the radio. We all
had an unspoken concern about how bad the
weather might be ahead.

By now there was nothing outside to look at except the blackness, so I turned my attention to the instrument panel. Most of the gauges were familiar to me. Only one or two were new since my active flying days. The soft glow of the panel lights provided a comforting relief from the otherwise bleak darkness. Except for one troubling thing: The light behind one of the instruments would regularly surge to a greater brightness than the others, then return to its normal glow. "A loose bulb," I thought. No, it couldn't be that. A loose bulb would flicker off and then come back on. This looked as if it was receiving a regular surge of too much power. "Something is wrong with the lighting system," I thought. "What'll we do up here in these clouds if those instrument lights go off? Maybe there's something wrong with the generator. Maybe there's something wrong with the whole electrical system!"

Realizing that my imagination was running away with me, I turned to the pilot and blurted out, "What's wrong with the light behind that instrument?"

"Nothing," he said. "As a matter of fact every time you see that little surge of extra light it means that somebody down there loves us!" Relieved, I asked for an explanation. "The instrument," he said, "is a transponder. When I filed my instrument flight plan they gave us a special number which no other plane aloft has. I put the number into the instrument by setting these little dials right there. Now the ground radar can identify us from other planes in the air. The little 'sensing light' that you see surges brighter every time the radar beam strikes our plane. It means that they have us in view on their radar screen, and that they know where we are. It also means we can call them and have them tell us where we are in case we don't know!"

Fascinated, I now anticipated each little surge of light from the instrument. What a difference a little information had made to me! What had caused fear and concern before now brought deep reassurances that somebody down there did love us, and that we were not nearly so alone as I had thought. It seemed desperately important that somebody was watching us, knew where we were, and cared what happened to us.

Anticipating my next question, the pilot added, "When their signal begins to weaken as we move to the limits of their range, they will pass us on to the next radar station near Chattanooga, where the same identification number will already be known to them. They'll watch us until they pass us on to the Knoxville station, and then they'll bring us to your home field."

I watched them watch us all the way home. I never tired of seeing the little light surge when the plane was touched by the radar beam. During the process of switching to the next station along the line I missed the reassurance of the "sensing light's" warmth. But when it came back again from the new source, it was even more precious to behold.

No, the Christian's life is not a mere reading of impersonal written gauges, devoid of warmth or feeling. The Holy Spirit in the believer's body is like that "sensing light" in the transponder, assuring us again and again that we are seen, that God knows where we are, and that He loves us very much. To accomplish this surge of confirming love ". . . His Holy Spirit speaks to us deep in our hearts, and tells us that we really are God's children."[1] "And because we are his sons God has sent the Spirit of his Son into our hearts, so now we can rightly speak of God as our dear Father. . . . And since we are his sons, everything he has belongs to us, for that is the way God planned."[2] "He has put his brand upon us—his mark of ownership—and given us his Holy Spirit in our hearts as guarantee that we belong to him, and as the first installment of all that he is going to give us."[3]

Jesus said, "I am the light of the world: he that followeth me shall not walk in darkness, but shall have the light of life!"[4] When one receives Jesus Christ within, the lasting presence of the Holy Spirit brings an enduring light that never goes out. Jesus said, "Be sure of this—that I am with you always, even to the end of the world."[5] For me the comforting and hopeful light of God's love has been softly glowing from the pages of God's Book for well over twenty years. But, oh, how blessed have been the soft strokes of God's radar on my life, bringing special surges of the warm knowledge of His care, His power, His forgiveness, His acceptance, His guidance and His presence. In recent years the surges have most often come from my realization of His wonderful, perfect character, and of the fact that He always responds to me and my need consistent with His perfect character.

At times those special "sensing light" experiences have resulted from the kind and thoughtful acts of friends, from answered prayer, or from watching God's sweet life-changing grace at work in a new believer's life. Of late the overwhelming beauty and balance of creation have echoed in my life the words of the Psalmist, "The heavens are telling the glory of God; they are a marvelous display of his craftsmanship. Day and night they keep on telling about God. Without a sound or word, silent in the skies, their message reaches out to all the world."[6]

And who is in a better position to enjoy the breathtaking and spectacular creation of God than those who fly? I remember flying alone one day, looking out in wonder at the vast reaches of space and thinking to myself, "If this universe does end out there somewhere, what does it end up against, and what would you call that against which it ended?" No answer to that, is there? Except to gasp with awe as you recall that the Creator is far greater than His creation, and to be comforted by the "sensing light" reminder that He is a God of love and that "Not one sparrow (What do they cost? Two for a penny?) can fall to the ground without your Father knowing it. And the very hairs of your head are all numbered. So don't worry! You are more valuable to him than many sparrows."[7] Surely no believer in Jesus Christ can help but be deeply affected by those glorious words.

Perhaps even now you have sensed the timely sweep of God's radar over your life, assuring you that somebody out there (and in here) loves you and cares about you and has you in plane view. The range of man's radar is limited, but God's care is not. "Out of his glorious, unlimited resources he will give you the mighty inner strengthening of his Holy Spirit. And I pray that Christ will be more and more at home in your hearts, living within you as you trust in him. . . . And may you be able to feel and understand, as all God's children should, how long, how wide, how deep, and how high his love really is; and to experience this love for yourselves, though it is so great that you will never see the end of it or fully know or understand it. And so at last you will be filled up with God himself."[8]

In an airplane it's a great reassurance to have the comfort of a working transponder. But in life we have greater assurance in our God who is the great Re-sponder! As Hosea puts it: "Oh, that we might know the Lord! Let us press on to know him, and he will respond to us as surely as the coming of dawn or the rain of early spring."[9]

But your experience of God's love is not to be an end in itself, but a means to another end which God has in view. He cares for you and me, but He cares equally for others. He wants you to share your experience of His love with others, first by your life style, and secondly, by your expressed and active concern for the well-being of others.

Notes

1. Romans 8:16, *The Living Bible*
2. Galatians 4:6,7, *TLB*
3. II Corinthians 1:22, *TLB*
4. John 8:12, *King James Version*
5. Matthew 28:20, *TLB*
6. Psalm 19:1-4, *TLB*
7. Matthew 10:29-31, *TLB*
8. Ephesians 3:16-19, *TLB*
9. Hosea 6:3, *TLB*

The Automatic Pilot

CHAPTER 9

It's a spooky thing to watch an automatic pilot function. You select the direction you want to fly and the altitude, make your power settings, turn on the automatic pilot, take your hands off the controls and, behold, the plane flies itself. If you drift a bit off your heading, the wheel turns, the plane banks, and then straightens out again when back on course. If you get below your proper altitude the steering column pulls back until the right altitude is attained, then it pushes over into straight and level flight. (All this with nobody touching it.) It's like watching an old player piano bang out a tune, as invisible fingers play the keys! But an automatic pilot has a safety factor not needed on a player piano. The human pilot always can overpower the automatic pilot and reassume control of the aircraft when the situation demands it. When turbulence comes and it becomes difficult to maintain the assigned altitude and course, some pilots prefer to let

the auto-pilot chase the needles on the gauges rather than to struggle with it themselves.

In flights of several hours' duration it can be most restful to the pilot to have the plane flown for him automatically. All the tedious work of flying has been taken out of it for him. Still he must remain alert and aware of the operation of the plane.

In many ways the surrendering of one's life to Jesus Christ is like putting a plane on auto-pilot. In effect, one removes hands and feet from the wheel and rudder pedals of his own life and says to the Holy Spirit within, "You fly it from here on." The big difference is that the Holy Spirit is personal, and a piece of machinery is not. But the basic idea is the same. The purpose of the Holy Spirit in the believer's heart is to keep him on the course of God's selection and at the altitude He determines. Anyone who has asked God really to take over, has experienced the same mysterious sensation that a pilot does when he lets the unseen auto-pilot take over. In my own life I have seen the hand of God directing my affairs, so that I could only sit back and marvel at what was happening.

He has demonstrated time and again that He can run my life so much better than I can; yet I am constantly amazed that I keep grabbing the controls and taking over from Him. God allows us to overpower His direction of our lives just as a pilot can overpower the auto-pilot. I suppose He permits this so that we can learn, as quickly as possible, that life is much happier and more fruitful when we let Him run it His way. We should know from the beginning, one would think, that One who loved us so much that He died for us, could only direct us in the best way. Yet that is a truth most Christians keep relearning from day to day. We struggle over the controls—first letting Him run it, then taking over for ourselves—messing up, losing our way, getting dangerously low; then, in a panic, asking Him to please take over again and put us back on the right track. His patience with us is amazing! As the Psalmist declared, "The Lord is good and glad to teach the proper path to all who go astray; he will teach the ways that are right and best to those who humbly turn to him. And when we obey him, every path he guides us on is fragrant with his lovingkindness and his truth."[1]

God's purpose in taking over the direction of our lives is twofold. First, He wants to change us on the inside and thus change our entire life-style. Paul puts it this way: "For God is at work within you, helping you want to obey him, and then helping you do what he wants."[2] We all would like to have the following qualities in our lives: LOVE, JOY, PEACE, PATIENCE, KINDNESS, GOODNESS, FAITHFULNESS, GENTLENESS AND SELF-CONTROL! The Bible says, "When the Holy Spirit controls our lives he will produce this kind of fruit in us."[3] To get these qualities in, God has to persuade us that the opposite qualities must be pushed out. Needless to say this takes time. And it takes some considerable willingness and cooperation on our part in order to let God have His way in us.

"But when you follow your own wrong inclinations your lives will produce these evil results: impure thoughts, eagerness for lustful pleasure, idolatry, spiritism (that is, encouraging the activity of demons), hatred and fighting, jealousy and anger, constant effort to get the best for yourself, complaints and criticisms, the feeling that everyone else is wrong except those in your own little group—and there will be wrong doctrine, envy, murder, drunkenness, wild parties, and all that sort of thing."[4] Furthermore, we are warned, ". . . that anyone living that sort of life will not inherit the kingdom of God."[5] It is because all of us are naturally inclined in this evil direction that we need the internal piloting of the Holy Spirit automatically steering us away from, and elevating us above, such a level of existence. That's why Paul wrote, "I advise you to obey only the Holy Spirit's instructions. He will tell you where to go and what to do, and then you won't always be doing the wrong things your evil nature wants you to do."[6]

Secondly, this internal change of life that is produced when your heart is put under the Holy Spirit's control will inevitably change both your attitude and action where other people are concerned. It is as simple as this: You'll begin to care about others! And you'll be prepared to do something to aid them in both their spiritual and physical needs. Jesus said, "Love each other just as much as I love you. Your strong love for each other will prove to the world that you are my disciples."[7] The name of the game is love in human relationships. It begins in the home, and extends to your job, civic responsibility and leisure time. The Christian life begins and continues with an intimate and honest relationship with Jesus Christ, but it must extend into other relationships where you meet and are involved with people.

The prerequisite for involvement with others, in honesty and in love, is to learn to care for (love) yourself first in the same way. The Bible says, "God showed his great love for us by sending Christ to die for us while we were still sinners. . . . When we were utterly helpless with no way of escape, Christ came at just the right time and died for us sinners who had no use for Him."* Get a good grip on this startling truth! God's love is demonstrated by His acceptance of us *as we are*. He accepts us *in spite of what we are*, and not because of what we are.

To care for (love) yourself is to *accept yourself as you are*, facing the truth honestly about both your vices and your virtues. Here I would say, no, God is not going to let you remain the way you are. By taking over your life from the inside, He intends to change you so that you "should become like his son."* *You don't change in order to come to God, you come to God in order to be changed*. As stated by a prisoner writing from jail: "Finally I see it! God doesn't change us in order to love us. He loves us in order to change us!" (Written to me by a black prisoner in the Dade County Jail, Miami, Florida. He had only four years of education.) It is this kind of loving acceptance from God that gives us the ability to accept ourselves as the unique, original persons for whom Christ died. Loving others begins with our acceptance of them as they are. God alone is in the people-changing business.

One of the great disciplines of military flight training is formation flying, that is, planes flying in close relationship to one another in the air at high speeds. The danger of mid-air collision with other planes in the formation is ever present. Crucial to good formation flying is a flight leader who flies smoothly, making changes in altitude, direction and speed with a deliberation born of the knowledge that by the time the alteration in attitude is known to the last man in the formation his reaction time has to be greatly reduced. Living the Christian life in relationship to others is very much like formation flying. You have your eye on the Leader (Jesus Christ), but you must always fly (your life) with your relationship to others in plane view. Like flying, both your well-being and theirs depend upon this kind of mutual concern for one another. The formation is large, and purely individualistic stunting can make quick shambles of it. Take your eyes off the Leader and those around you, and you are already on your way to real trouble.

An automatic pilot has limitations. It flies the course for which it is set without regard to other planes in the air. But the Holy Spirit in the believer's heart majors in making you sensitive both to the presence and the need of others all about you. Almost every great work of compassion in the world today was either begun by someone who had turned his life over to Jesus Christ, or was the result of someone imitating the example of a Christian who had begun such a work. Hospitals began out of Christian concern during the religious madness of the Crusades. The labor union movement began for the purpose of protecting the exploited worker. The concern to start it was born when Jesus Christ took over the heart of a working man. The concern for the poor and the needy, the sick and the dying, had its origins in the Bible and from the spoken words of the Lord Jesus Christ.

The purpose of Christ is not for you to go out and start some new grand work of compassion, but rather to have you show His love and concern for those with whom you come in contact in your day-to-day life. The encouraging word, the helpful hand, the need met, evokes from Christ these beautiful words, "For I was hungry and you fed me; I was thirsty and you gave me water; I was a stranger and you invited me into your home; naked and you clothed me; sick and in prison, and you visited me. . . . When you did it to these my brothers you were doing it to me!"[10]

When the Holy Spirit pilots and controls your life the needs of those around you automatically come into plane view, and that same spirit directs you to meet those needs.

But there is more, much more, to be seen from the vantage point of the Christian who is lifted off into the heavens.

Notes

1. Psalm 25:8-10, *The Living Bible*
2. Philippians 2:13, *TLB*
3. Galatians 5:22,23, *TLB*
4. Galatians 5:19-21, *TLB*
5. Galatians 5:21, *TLB*
6. Galatians 5:16, *TLB*
7. John 13:34,35, *TLB*
8. Romans 5:8,6, *TLB*
9. Romans 8:29, *TLB*
10. Matthew 25:35,36,40, *TLB*

On a Clear Day You Can See Forever!

CHAPTER 10

The little fighter plane was struggling, full power, full rpm (revolutions per minute), in an awkward nose-high attitude, but unable to gain another foot of altitude. The reason? I had flown it to the limits of its operational capabilities. With the permission of the squadron engineering officer, I had taken off with the intention of seeing how high it would fly, and now I had reached the limit. It figured out to be something over forty-two thousand feet, eight miles above sea level.

The spiraling climb up had been boring, and the last ten thousand feet had been tedious and slow. But the ultimate view was breathtaking, and well worth the effort. My flight had originated at the Naval Air Station in Klamath Falls, Oregon, and the city now lay directly below me. It was one of those really clear days in the year 1944 P.P. (pre-pollution). In the distance to the west of me I could see

a bit of the Pacific Ocean; to the immediate north of me that magnificent jewel of unbelievable blue, Crater Lake; to the east of me the stretches of the desert regions of southeastern Oregon and the edge of Idaho; to the south of me, in California, the beauty of snowcapped Mount Shasta.

The horizon in every direction showed the gentle, but definite curvature of the earth. Above me I could see eternal distance out into space. In those days I was not much given to the mystical, but this was overwhelming. I had the distinct feeling that I did not wish to return to earth, much as I knew I must. My horizons had been pushed back, and the glorious creation all around me gripped the core of my being. The song written years later best describes what I sensed: "On a Clear Day You Can See Forever!" For me the whole world seemed to be in plane view.

(Yet for all the impressiveness of the experience, a return to the earth put everything back into the same old perspective that I'd known before the flight. There were the same old jealousies in the squadron, the same bickering, the same lusting and partying, the same insecurities and fears.)

Similarly, when I was lifted into the heavenlies with Jesus Christ, I began to get a plane view of life, of myself and of others that started a change in me which is still in progress. As a result of His Spirit in my life my perspective on everything has changed, is changing, and shall be changed even more in the future. Paul put it this way, "When someone becomes a Christian he becomes a brand new person inside. He is not the same any more. A new life has begun!'" It means that I began to see things from a new and exciting perspective. Matters that were baffling and obscure before began to emerge into plane view.

It is as though the Christian begins to see things in the overview from above—from God's perspective. Jumbled facts and situations begin to fit together like a giant jigsaw puzzle. Disjointed events of history begin to show their spiritual relationship to one another, and the pattern of the divine plan emerges into sensible shape. When this happens the Christian's heart whispers, "It's true! The Lord God Omnipotent reigns! and, somehow I'm beginning to see where I fit into it all!" The reason for this has nothing to do with the brilliance of the believer, but rather with the presence of the Holy Spirit in the believer's heart and mind.

"But we know about these things because God has sent his Spirit to tell us and his Spirit searches out and shows us all of God's deepest secrets. . . . And God has actually given us his Spirit (not the world's spirit) to tell us about the wonderful free gifts of grace and blessing that God has given us. . . . But the spiritual man has insight into everything, and that bothers and baffles the man of the world, who can't understand him at all. . . . But strange as it seems, we Christians actually do have within us a portion of the very thoughts and mind of Christ."[2] Let's look at some of the things His Spirit brings into plane view for the Christian.

The grand and majestic sweep of God's master plan in human history becomes discernible even in the tangled mass of evil events for which men and nations are responsible. The Bible says that God can even cause the wrath of man to bring Him praise.[3] God began it all, and God will end it all on His schedule. "I am the A and Z, the Beginning and the Ending of all things, says God, who is the Lord, the All Powerful One who is, and was, and is coming again!"[4] Time and again in history we see the truth of God's plan at work in the lives of men and of nations. The quality of life man creates is determined by his response to the sober offer of God, found in Deuteronomy, "Behold, I set before you this day a blessing and a curse; a blessing, if ye obey the commandments of the Lord your God, which I command you this day; and a curse, if ye will not obey the commandments of the Lord your God, but turn aside out of the way which I command you this day, to go after other gods, which ye have not known."[5] Life is not as Shakespeare wrote, "A tale told by an idiot, full of sound and fury and signifying nothing."[6] It only seems that way when men disregard the commandments of God.

The pathetic history of Israel told in the Old Testament is the classic illustration of what has been endlessly repeating itself in all other nations of the world ever since. "And with a breath he can scatter the plans of all the nations who oppose him, but his own plan stands forever. His intentions are the same for every generation."[7] Happiness and purpose are found in obedience. Misery and meaninglessness are found in disobedience.

But the plane view found through Jesus Christ is not limited merely to an understanding of what is producing the present turmoil, and what God's an-

106

swer for it is. God's revelation in the Bible tells us that the God and Father of Jesus Christ is also the Creator of this universe and all that is in it. He is the First Cause of this magnificently complex creation: galaxies and the heavens in their overwhelming order, so vast that the distances must be measured in light years; and this earth, its building blocks so small that they remain invisible to the microscopic eye, yet so perfect in their order and purpose that their presence is attested to through experiments.

"By faith—by believing God—we know that the world and the stars—in fact, all things—were made at God's command; and that they were all made from things that can't be seen."[8] The evolutionary theory must believe that all of this created order is some sort of happy accident! And that demands a wilder, blinder leap of faith than to accept at face value the words of Jesus who says, "But from the beginning of the creation God made them male and female. . . ."[9] Don't get suckered in on the so-called scientific proof for the evolutionary theory. Proof is sadly lacking. I thank God that in our day there are many volumes available casting great shadows of scientific doubt over this alleged proof. The academic credentials of those producing these books are above question.[10] It has been my experience to discover that opponents of biblical creationism usually try to win the day by ridicule rather than by reasonable arguments citing the scientific facts. The Bible says, "He (God) merely spoke, and the heavens were formed, and all the galaxies of stars. . . . For when he but spoke, the world began! It appeared at his command!"[11] But so commanding are those facts that some states are giving serious consideration to demanding equal time be given to the teaching of the theory of creation as well as the theory of evolution.

But actually, isn't the evolutionary theory just another part of a larger desire to do away with the whole idea of a moral Creator God? Only by getting rid of God as the explanation of the origin of the universe can man complete his rebellion against his Maker. It is reported that when Karl Marx read the theory of Charles Darwin, he exclaimed, "At last! The system is complete! Now I have a way to get rid of God as the First Cause!"[12] It is peculiar the way we transitory men indulge in all manner of mental gymnastics in order to maintain our rebellion against the only source of hope and help available in this crazy mixed-up world. How long can we maintain this fiction of our self-sufficiency? Why not admit our need?

A Christian is a person who has a plane view of his own need. There are so many things in this life that we can't handle. Why continue to pretend we can? There are so many things we would like to be and aren't. So many times we're anxious and afraid when we know we shouldn't be. There are so many times of discouragement and emptiness, loneliness and estrangement, guilt and suffering. Why pretend to one another that this is not so? Why deceive ourselves with the passé "stiff upper lip" routine?

The follower of Jesus Christ has a plane view of his ongoing needs and he does not try to deny their reality. But he has a gracious source of help—God. The Word of God encourages him to bring all those needs to the Lord whether they be big or small. "The Lord is close to those whose hearts are breaking; he rescues those who are humbly sorry for their sins. The good man does not escape all troubles—he has them too. But the Lord helps him in each and every one."[13] All God desires is an admission of our need and we can count on Him to deliver the strength required. Jesus said to the apostle Paul at a time of personal crisis, ". . . I am with you; that is all you need. My power shows up best in weak people."[14] We admit our weakness, and the source of power and deliverance comes into plane view. As a new Christian wrote me from a prison where he had found Jesus, "I don't mean to say that all my problems are solved, it's just that now I am able to look on them from a different side!"

It becomes increasingly evident to the Spirit-filled believer that God is not only the Creator and the Controller of this world, but that He is also the One who will consummate all things in His own way and in His own time. He will finally bring this world as we know it to an end. The Christian then, regardless of when he lives in history, always has the end in plane view. Sometimes a pilot on short flights, on clear days and, at the right altitude, can have both his point of origin and his destination in view at the same time. The Christian, in spite of how long his life-trip, always can keep his point of origin and the final destination of both himself and the world in plane view. How? By simply taking at face value the clear words of the Bible concerning this subject. We have the specifics of what life will be like in the last days.

Paul said, "You may as well know this too . . . that in the last days it is going to be very difficult to be a Christian. For people will love only themselves and their money; they will be proud and boastful, sneering at God, disobedient to their parents, ungrateful to them, and thoroughly bad. They will be hardheaded and never give in to others; they will be constant liars and troublemakers and will think nothing of immorality. They will be rough and cruel, and sneer at those who try to be good. They will betray their friends; they will be hotheaded, puffed up with pride, and prefer good times to worshiping God. They will go to church, yes, but they won't really believe anything they hear. Don't be taken in by people like that."[15]

The Lord Jesus spoke so clearly of things that could only be related to our time in history that it will make the hairs stand up on the back of your neck. He said, " 'They (the Jews) will be brutally killed by enemy weapons, or sent away as exiles and captives to all the nations of the world (fulfilled in A.D. 70); and Jerusalem shall be conquered and trampled down by the Gentiles (non-Jewish people) until the period of Gentile triumph ends in God's good time. (In 1967 the Jews recaptured all of Jerusalem for the first time since long before those words were spoken.) Then there will be strange events in the skies—warnings, evil omens and portents in the sun, moon and stars (Neil Armstrong set foot on the moon in 1969); and down here on earth the nations will be in turmoil, perplexed by the roaring seas and strange tides. (Recent Gulf Coast tidal waves, plus the tidal disaster at the Bay of Bengal, exceed in severity anything in the history of those areas.) The courage of many people will falter because of the fearful fate they see coming upon the earth, for the stability of the very heavens will be broken up. (Could this point toward pollution either from atomic fallout or just plain air pollution? See also Revelation 9:18.) Then the peoples of the earth shall see me, the Messiah, coming in a cloud with power and great glory. So when all these things begin to happen, stand straight and look up! For your salvation is near!' Then he gave them this illustration: 'Notice the fig tree, or any other tree. When the leaves come out, you know without being told that summer is near. In the same way, when you see the events taking place that I've described you can be just as sure that the Kingdom of God is near. I solemnly declare to you that when these things happen, the end of this age has come. And though all heaven and earth shall pass away, yet my words remain forever true. Watch out! Don't let my sudden coming catch you unawares; don't let me find you living in careless ease, carousing and drinking, and occupied with the problems of this life, like all the rest of the world. Keep a constant watch. And pray that if possible you may arrive in my presence without having to experience these horrors'."[16]

When you add to that the statement of Jesus, in Matthew, about famine, wars and earthquakes, and look out on the world scene with its endless wars, increase of earthquakes and threat of serious world famine, you can only marvel at the convergence of all these events in our time in history.

The Bible is full of indications that the nation of Israel will be reconstituted in the land as an independent people during the end times. It has happened, and the magnitude of the military victories which this tiny nation has achieved, against all odds, rivals any victories of ancient Israel in Bible times. They have rebuilt the waste places even as the Bible said they would, restoring the old ruins and causing the desert to blossom like the rose.[17]

It is true, every generation from New Testament times until now has had among them those that felt that the return of Jesus Christ was imminent. But it is also true that this generation now alive is beginning to see a convergence of Bible prophecy fulfillment more detailed and sweeping than any other time in history. My suggestion is that each individual study the Scriptures for himself, and then be persuaded in his own mind as to whether or not the end is in plane view.

None of us likes to think about the end whether it be personal or collective. In spite of the fact that we either see or hear of persons whose lives have ended every day, we do everything possible to crowd out any thought of death happening to us. But the Christian who has been lifted off into the heavenlies, with Jesus Christ, has a startling fact to hang on to, which casts the whole matter in a new perspective. For him life is eternal now as well as later. Jesus said, "How earnestly I tell you this—anyone who believes in me already has eternal life!"[18] When the living Christ enters a person by His Holy Spirit, a new quality of life is imparted to the believ-

112

er and experienced now. It's like the difference between taxiing a plane around on the ground and taking to the air. A whole new dimension of things has been introduced. A new liberty with new possibilities arising out of a new set of values comes into view. A personal potential which has limits sheds those restrictions as God challenges the believer with His invitation, "Call unto me, and I will answer thee, and shew thee great and mighty things, which thou knowest not."[19] Despite what the critics say, Christianity is not merely "pie in the sky by and by." It is eternal life here and now!

Yes, the Christian dies in his body. The Bible has a ready explanation for that. "Yet, even though Christ lives within you, your body will die because of sin; but your spirit will live, for Christ has pardoned it."[20] The last vestige of sin dies with the body and our spirits are brought into the presence of the One who pardoned us through His death and bodily resurrection.

No pilot deceives himself about the success of his flight until he has landed safely at his final destination, parked his plane and shut off his engines. No matter how successful the takeoff, how precise the navigation or how pleasant the flight, when he is on that final approach he knows it is how his plane meets the ground that determines his success or failure. Many a seemingly successful flight has ended in tragedy on the final landing. The supremely critical times in flying are on lift-off and landing.

So also in life. What point to the successful life, if it crashes at the ultimate destination—death. The believer in Jesus Christ makes the entire journey

113

with the happy confidence that he will be brought to his final destination in safety. He makes his final approach homing on the soothing and certain words of his Saviour: "Let not your heart be troubled. You are trusting God, now trust in me. There are many homes up there where my Father lives, and I am going to prepare them for your coming. When everything is ready, then I will come and get you, so that you can always be with me where I am. If this weren't so, I would tell you plainly. And you know where I am going and how to get there."

"No, we don't," Thomas said. "We haven't any idea where you are going, so how can we know the way?" Jesus told him, "I am the Way—yes, and the Truth and the Life. No one can get to the Father except by means of me."[21]

A recent flying experience reemphasized to me the Christian's assurance when facing death. I had just finished a crusade in Wilkes County, North Carolina, and a friend flew me home to Knoxville, in a beautiful twin-engined, prop-jet executive aircraft. Just after we crossed the Smoky Mountains into the Tennessee Valley we ran into weather that was pure "soup." The airport was still open but the visibility and ceiling were right at the minimum operating standards. John, the pilot, informed me we'd be making an instrument approach; that is, we would land by instruments, not by sight.

Following the instructions from the ground, John, making the prescribed turns and descents, turned to me and said, "We're on final, it won't be long." At that point we could not see a thing except the swirling clouds that made our own wing tips hazy. The blind descent toward an earth we could not see, made a few seconds seem like "too long." In vain I looked down, maybe I'd see a tree, but none came in view. Then John said softly, "Look!"

Instinctively I looked forward. There, glowing radiantly through the clouds, was a long brilliant pathway of light. A string of strobe lights straight down the middle of the pathway flashed in quick succession, from the point nearest us right down to where the light path met the runway. The quick repetition of the flashing gave the warmest sense of beckoning, as if to say, "This way, this way, this way is home!"

As we drew closer I could see a short cross-bar of lights about three-fourths of the way down the light path—it made a magnificent sight—a beautiful, warm, beckoning cross! Beyond it lay the runway that meant I was home. I turned to the pilot, "Look, John, the way of the cross leads home!"

He nodded and said, "It sure does!" John only days before had found his spiritual home, by yielding his life to Jesus Christ. I had been a Christian for years and I was thinking of that final home that Jesus has prepared for me. In a new way it had come into plane view. The way of the cross leads home. It wasn't a clear day, but I could see forever.

But there is even more. "And if the Spirit of God, who raised up Jesus from the dead, lives in you, he will make your dying bodies live again after you die, by means of this same Holy Spirit living in you."²² Think of it! a new perfect body, never again subject to pain, sin, sorrow or death. Compare such a bright and sure prospect as that, with

115

the unmixed horror which faces the unbeliever. For him life is finally an abject futility which has no more meaning than that his body is shut up in a box, and put into the ground to rot, not to mention the possibility of his spirit spending an eternity in hell. A deadening feeling of fear can't help but leak through into any life that faces such a dreary future. Contrast that with the living hope which the Christian has, plus the fact that the Holy Spirit within confirms that the hope is true.

God has put His plan into plane view. It is yours to participate in and to enjoy. From the moment that you take off and begin lifting upwards in Christ to a new plane of life, you can see the mighty plan of God unfolding in history, in creation, and in yourself. And you are assured that this wonderful experience into which you have ventured is going to consummate either in your safe death, or in Jesus Christ's physical return to earth. Either way heaven is your ultimate destination. You are free to overfly the mountains of difficulty, penetrate clouds of sin and to ride out the storms of life now that Christ is in you! He is your hope of glory.

John wrote, "Beloved ones, we are God's children now, and what we shall be has not yet been shown; but we know that when He appears we shall resemble Him, for we shall see Him as He is."[23]

Finally, the Lord God Himself: *in plane view!*

Notes

1. II Corinthians 5:17, *The Living Bible*
2. I Corinthians 2:10,12,15,16, *TLB*
3. Psalm 76:10, *TLB*
4. Revelation 1:8, *TLB*

5. Deuteronomy 11:26-28, *King James Version*
6. *Macbeth,* Act 5, scene 4 (Shakespeare)
7. Psalm 33:10,11, *TLB*
8. Hebrews 11:3, *TLB*
9. Mark 10:6, *TLB*
10. For bibliography write to:
    Dr. John M. Moore, Managing Editor
    Creation Research Society Quarterly
    2717 Cranbrook Road
    Ann Arbor, Michigan 48104
11. Psalm 33:6,9, *TLB*
12. Picked up in a lecture, but unable to discover the source.
13. Psalm 34:18,19, *TLB*
14. II Corinthians 12:9, *TLB*
15. II Timothy 3:1-5, *TLB*
16. Luke 21:24-36, *TLB*
17. Isaiah 58:12; 61:4; Ezekiel 36:33-36, *KJV*
18. John 6:47, *TLB*
19. Jeremiah 33:3, *KJV*
20. Romans 8:10, *TLB*
21. John 14:1-6, *TLB*
22. Romans 8:11, *TLB*
23. I John 3:2, *The New Berkeley Version in Modern English*

DATE DUE